Howard **.eton** is an amateur baker from Sheffield who first began baking as a child. is passionate about being inclusive in his baking, creating food for the specifi dietary needs of his mum and dad and the incredibly challenging birthday c e requests of his nieces. As a contestant on the fourth series of the BBC's *The* *Great British Bake Off*, he immediately caught the public's attention with his fir bake – a gluten-free passion fruit and coconut sandwich cake. More recently he as been demonstrating his creative approach to gluten-free baking at numero food festivals and shows, teaching at Hartingtons artisan food school in Bakewe England, and has been a brand ambassador for Newburn Bakehous the gluten-free wing of Warburtons bakery. His engaging personality nd quirky sense of humour has made him a popular guest panellist on *Bake O* spin-off show, *An Extra Slice*.

Also available from Constable & Robinson

Everyday Lebanese Cooking
Everyday Thai Cooking
Everyday Curries
Everyday Cooking for One
Everyday Bread from Your Bread Machine
How To Make Perfect Panini
How To Make Your Own Cordials and Syrups
The Healthy Slow Cooker Cookbook
Traditional Country Preserving
Southern Italian Family Cooking
Afternoon Tea
Pâtisserie
A Lebanese Feast of Vegetables, Pulses, Herbs and Spices

DELICIOUS GLUTEN-FREE BAKING

Howard Middleton

A How To Book

ROBINSON

ROBINSON

First published in Great Britain in 2015 by Robinson

A CIP catalogue record for this book
is available from the British Library.

ISBN: 978-1-47213-586-5 (paperback)
ISBN: 978-1-47213-587-2 (ebook)

Typeset in Great Britain by Mousemat Design Limited, www.mousematdesign.com
Printed and bound in China

Robinson
is an imprint of
Constable & Robinson Ltd
Carmelite House
50 Victoria Embankment
London EC4Y 0DZ

An Hachette UK Company
www.hachette.co.uk

www.littlebrown.co.uk

How To Books are published by Constable & Robinson, a part of Little, Brown Book Group. We welcome proposals from
authors who have first-hand experience of their subjects. Please set out the aims of your book, its target market and its
suggested contents in an email to Nikki.Read@howtobooks.co.uk

With love to Peter – my biggest critic
and my best friend

CONTENTS

INTRODUCTION

We all crave what we cannot have. It's a fact that things that seem out of our reach often become far more desirable. And the same is true for people with dietary restrictions. Past indifference to a little baguette has the potential to grow into nothing less than a magnificent obsession.

This book includes recipes for the things people have told me they crave – chewy, crusty bread, light luscious cakes and a decent doughnut. These recipes are here to satisfy and pacify. But good gluten-free baking is about more than simply emulating standard wheat- flour bakes – it's about realising the potential of the alternative.

There's just so much out there – including ideas from other cuisines that traditionally use non-wheat flours and have some wonderful gluten-free dishes. I hope you'll find things in this book that satisfy your cravings, but I also hope you are encouraged to venture further afield and discover new delights.

FÖR REDNING   OCH BAKNING

KOCKENS

En ren naturprodukt från svenska odlare

Lyckeby
Potatis

POLENTA

Hemp

GLUTEN-FREE BAKING INGREDIENTS

Before you put on your pinny, let's look at the ingredients for gluten-free baking. Starting with an introduction to gluten-free flours, we'll then look at other essentials for your cupboards. I'll go on to highlight a few of the things you'll need to keep an eye out for, and finish with a few words about baking for other 'free from' diets.

GLUTEN-FREE FLOURS

I get excited about flour. When it comes to trying out different varieties, I'm a self-confessed flour addict. Sadly, I'm also a bit of a flour snob – I've lost count of the number of times someone has proudly presented a gluten-free bake, I eagerly ask what flour they used, and they've replied, 'gluten-free'. Yes, the gluten-free plain and self-raising flour blends definitely have their place … but they really are only part of the picture.

Try pastry making with tapioca flour, and experience the crisp squeak of a trek through fresh fallen snow. Breathe in the musky, heady scent of hemp – sensory delights you wouldn't get if you only used flour blends (or standard wheat flour, for that matter).

This is not an exhaustive list – I'm discovering and trying new gluten-free flours all the time – but it's hopefully a taste of the huge variety, and a useful insight into their potential.

Cornflour

Once widely used in cakes and pastries, somewhere along the way cornflour was condemned to be used only for thickening sauces and custard. I call this a gravy miscarriage of justice. Its liberation is way overdue, so rather than dipping in for a teaspoon at a time, I buy boxes of the stuff. It's such an innocent, inoffensive but industrious little flour – beautifully light, and perfect in a fatless sponge cake or *Summer Swiss roll* (see page 96).

Whole grain cornflour (sometimes called maize flour) is less widely available – it's recognisably more yellow in colour. However, in its coarser form it's sold as cornmeal or polenta.

Gram flour

Made from chickpeas and also called besan flour, gram flour is a butter-hued beauty, widely used in Indian and South European dishes. Another absorbent flour, I find it works well in carrot cakes and makes classic batters, so is perfect for my *Socca* (see page 38) and *Red onion bhajis* (see page 120).

Millet flour

A fairly new entry to my flour jars, millet has actually been cultivated as a grain for centuries. Many will recognise this as the tiny pearl-like grain used for birdseed, but there are many varieties of millet, and it turns up in different forms in African, Indian and Far Eastern dishes. Its starchy quality helps with crumb texture, so I've introduced it in some of my pastry recipes and in the *Fresh blackberry and almond scones* (see page 56).

Potato flour

There's something about potato flour that makes me smile. Maybe it's because I buy a brand called *Kockens Potatismjöl*, which you can't really say without attempting an impression of a Swedish chef.

It works well in combination with other flours, so you'll often find it in commercial flour blends, and its absorbent, starchy quality is useful in recipes that contain wetter fruits, like plums. It's used quite a lot in traditional Scandinavian cooking (though frustratingly often along with wheat flour), and I've come up with a recipe for *Swedish butter biscuits*, or *uppåkra* (see page 78), which will let you play the Swedish chef again. Not surprisingly, potato flour works with fresh potatoes, too, as in my *Two-potato farls* (see page 32).

Rice flour

An accommodating flour, this has earned its place as the staple in many a gluten-free recipe. As with the grain itself, the taste of rice flour can be a little bland and, if you overdo it in a recipe, it can taste like the scum from a pan of boiled basmati, so it works best when it's teamed up with stronger flavours – a perfect foil for unusual flours or pungent spices. Brown rice and white rice flours are both readily available and pretty much interchangeable in recipes.

For a terrifically easy tempura batter, whisk egg whites until frothy, smear over vegetables or fish, then dunk in rice flour before frying.

Glutinous rice flour is quite a different animal – definitely the Marmite of rice flours. Its dense, sticky quality is not to everyone's taste but I think it's worth trying most things once, so have a go at the *Sticky rice crab cakes* (see page 130) and see what you think. And just in case you're confused by its name, it's glutinous but still gluten free.

Tapioca flour

Squeaky little tapioca flour is another team player that gets on well with others and features in commercial flour blends. A starch extracted from the cassava root, native to Brazil, tapioca flour turns up in Brazilian bakes, like their cheesy bread or *pão de queijo*. I use its impressive crustiness in my *Tapioca tapenade cobs* (see page 14).

Oat flour

Once out of bounds because of cross-contamination in production processes, truly gluten-free oat products are now becoming more widely available. Oat flour is impressively versatile. I also like the nubbly texture of pinhead oats, which make a gluten-free alternative to the malted wheat grains you get in granary bread. Both the oat flour and the pinhead oats are in my recipe for *Spiced pumpkin bread* (see page 16).

Amaranth flour

Amaranth's versatility is impressive. Like a *grande dame* of stage and screen, it has a wide repertoire – seeds, flour, flakes and puffed pops. With varieties grown for their ornamental flowers, amaranth can even provide its own bouquet at the end of the show. I applaud its range (and play up to its theatricality a little) by offering the flakes a part in my *Blue lavender and amaranth cake* (see page 62).

Chestnut flour

Mainly sourced from France, it's worth tracking down for its (perhaps not surprisingly) chestnut flavour. Popular in crêpes and to add flavour to (often sadly, wheaten) bread, I think there's something rather whimsical, almost magical, about the idea of making flour from chestnuts, so I like to use it in festive gluten-free bakes, like the *Black Forest brownies* (see page 170) and *Sticky figgy puddings* (see page 172).

Coconut flour

I've described other flours as absorbent, but coconut flour takes the biscuit (which undeniably it's very good in). As you'd expect, it has a great flavour, but it does have a knack of tightening bakes, sometimes beyond recognition. I recently tried replacing gram flour with coconut in some previously moist and delicious carrot cakes and ended up with a dozen little rock cakes that stubbornly refused to rise. In small quantities, however, it will help bind pastry without imparting a strong flavour, as in *Christmas in Bakewell* (see page 184).

Flaxseed flour

With strong binding properties, flaxseed is often used to replace eggs in vegan recipes. It has a slightly nutty taste and is highly nutritious. You can admire it flexing in my *No-nut breakfast bars* (see page 82).

Hemp flour

Ah, the infamous hemp flour – yes, it's from the cannabis family, but no, it's not narcotic. After decades of weaving textiles, hemp has recently re-emerged bleary-eyed from its attic studio to offer a growing range of seeds, oil, milk and flour (though this is so scarce you really need a reliable dealer). Dark sack-coloured and with a (I think not unpleasant) musky aroma, the flour can be found hanging out in *Amsterdam apple cake* (see page 60).

Nut flours

What Americans call almond meal, we Brits know best as ground almonds, so it may be harder for us to think of this as a flour, but it is. So in the alphabet of nut flours, let's not get stuck on the letter A, when you can also make flour from Brazil nuts, cobnuts, and so on. You'll occasionally see a packet of hazelnut flour in specialist shops and upmarket supermarkets, but invest in a nut grinder and the world is your cluster.

Quinoa flour

Not quite a cereal or grass, quinoa's edible seeds are most familiar as a grain in salads – the gluten-free alternative to couscous or bulgur wheat. It has a mild, nutty taste that lends itself to being pepped up with stronger flavours and spices, but is equally comfortable playing the part of comfort food – more recently emerging in flake form to rival porridge, popped like popcorn, and even as quinoa crisps. Quinoa flour is best used in a supporting role – adding a little nuttiness to sweet or savoury pastry. You'll find some in my *Seeded loaf* (see page 24), among others.

Sorghum flour

Like millet, sorghum has mainly been cultivated for animal feed but the variety used for humans produces a flour with a sweet, mild flavour and smooth texture. Not really suitable as a soloist, but sorghum flour works well with others in bread and pastry – it's in my *Plum and pecan pie with continental pastry* (see page 70).

Soya flour

I'll be as delicate as I can here. So many people complain about the flatulent qualities of soya (not just those eating it), that I've relegated it to a safe distance. Enough said.

Teff flour

Grassy teff helps create a good crust on a loaf of bread but I think its flavour can be overpowering. Fans of the British TV series *Dinnerladies* will recall the story of Auntie Margo eating a raffia drinks coaster thinking it was a high-fibre biscuit – if you're not looking to recreate this experience, you'd best keep teff in a cameo role.

Flour blends

Having said that commercial blends should not be the be-all and end-all of gluten-free baking, they are important. I use a gluten-free bread flour blend as the basis of most of my breads, but please try mixing things up with some of the other gluten-free flours out there.

Wheat-free flours

There are a number of flours that are classed as wheat free, but are not gluten free, such as barley and rye. 'Ancient' forms of wheat, like spelt and einkorn, are sometimes considered a potential alternative for those intolerant to modern wheat, but again these are **not** gluten-free, so they don't feature in the recipes in this book.

Flourless baking

Don't forget that not all baking includes flour in its ingredients. So-called flourless cakes are often nut-based (the tortes), but you'll also come across recipes that use cocoa powder in place of flour. Most roulade recipes are flourless (either cocoa or meringue-based) and meringues in general offer lots of potential in gluten-free baking.

GLUTEN-FREE ESSENTIALS
Yeast

Baking yeast doesn't contain gluten so you can use any kind you like without having to get a magnifying glass to the label. (Brewer's yeast can contain gluten, but hopefully you weren't thinking of using this.) I use quick yeast from Dove's Farm, which is also called fast-action dried yeast. You can buy it in tubs or packets, like I do, and it also comes in sachets, which contain 7g or about 1 1/2 tsp.

The other alternatives are ordinary dried yeast and fresh yeast. Ordinary dried yeast tends to have bigger granules than the quick yeast and is traditionally 'activated' with sugar and warm water before you mix your dough. I find it's really not necessary. Fresh yeast comes in blocks – use 5g in place of 1 tsp dried yeast and rub it into the flour to disperse it, like you do with butter when making pastry.

Coax the yeast to do its work by using lukewarm liquid and leaving it to rise in a fairly warm place, but never force it in too hot a spot. If you do, you'll discover that what goes up soon comes down.

Gluten-free baking powder

Essential to add lift to your baking (sorry, you knew that already), most baking powders use alternatives to wheat flour nowadays, but there are some that haven't changed their ways. Always use a baking powder labelled gluten free.

Bicarbonate of soda

A component of baking powder that's often used alone to produce a bubbly texture and as a raising agent, bicarbonate of soda isn't mixed with any flour products so it is gluten free.

Xanthan gum

A useful thickener that also helps prevent gluten-free cakes from sinking in the middle. It's become a staple in gluten-free baking but you can use guar gum if you prefer.

Guar gum

Strong stuff – guar gum is many times more powerful than cornflour at thickening liquids. A little goes a long way.

Psyllium husk powder

A great addition to gluten-free bread making, a few spoonfuls help to absorb moisture and produce a dough texture that's tighter and, well, basically more bread-like. Often sold as a product to aid digestion, its price can vary enormously, so shop around.

Polenta

Though I've already referred to polenta under cornflour, it's worth mentioning it again in its own right. Polenta adds crunch to savoury *Stilton and walnut biscuits* (see page 174), is good as a final crusty dusting on bread and will absorb excess moisture if you sprinkle it on a pastry case before filling.

Ground rice

A good alternative to semolina (which contains gluten) or even to ground almonds (though you may need to reduce the quantity), ground rice is to rice flour what polenta is to cornflour. Naturally gluten free, but check the packet, as a major brand currently warns theirs is not suitable for coeliacs because of production processes.

Spices

Having a good selection of spices is essential in all cookery, but if you're going to widen your horizons with gluten-free flours, you may as well be a bit more experimental with your flavourings too. Most commercial spice blends add salt – I prefer to be in control of this myself. The Spice Shop (www.thespiceshop.co.uk) is good for spices and blends that have no added salt and are all gluten free.

ONES TO WATCH
Alcohol

Fruit- and vegetable-based booze – like wine, brandy and vodka – should contain no gluten. It looks like the jury is still out on some grain-based drinks like whisky. Beer is traditionally brewed from malted barley, so it isn't gluten free, but there are gluten-free beers now available.

Blue cheese
The moulds that give cheeses like Stilton and Roquefort their distinctive blueness were traditionally cultivated on rye and wheat bread, so some people understandably think these cheeses are not truly gluten free. However, this gluten encounter is so distant in the cheeses' DNA (and scientific tests have also shown no detectable gluten) that most people consider them gluten free. If you are still sceptical, use a strong non-blue cheese instead.

Chocolate
To be honest, chocolate is a bit of a minefield. So much is produced in factories using nuts, most chocolate contains some dairy products and you'll even occasionally see wrapper warnings about gluten. Dedicated manufacturers are now producing chocolate that is guaranteed gluten free, dairy free and nut free, so look out for this.

Food colourings
Food colourings shouldn't contain gluten but always check to see if there's a warning about cross-contamination from production processes.

Pickles, relishes and chutneys
Some manufacturers use malt vinegar that contains barley and wheat-based thickeners, so check the label for any potential allergens.

Soy sauce
Most soy sauce contains wheat, so look for one like Clearspring's Organic Tamari that's rice-based and is labelled gluten free.

Stock cubes
Many leading brands' cubes contain wheat and gluten, so go for one like Kallo that uses maize starch and is gluten and lactose free.

Sugar decorations
Don't be seduced by a little razzle dazzle – always check labels on sugar decorations to make sure they're gluten free. Little silver balls, for example, sometimes contain wheat, but there are brands available that don't.

DAIRY-FREE INGREDIENTS
Most 'free from' ranges nowadays are predominantly gluten free, but they include some dairy-free products too. I've tried to take the same approach with this book – offering suggestions for dairy-free options where I can.

Non-dairy 'milks' like soya milk are readily available and the choice is widening, with almond, coconut and gluten-free oat milk. I prefer hemp milk or oat milk to soya for general use (many say they're more digestible) and I like to play up the individual flavours of the nut milks, as I've done with the hazelnut milk in the recipe for *Hazel flann* (see page 142).

In most of the recipes where I've used butter, you can substitute this with a dairy-free olive or sunflower spread, like Pure. Because of the water content, you may need a little less fat in the pastry recipes, but it should make no difference in cakes.

Cheese is trickier – although there are tofu-based vegan alternatives to cheese available, they don't always behave the same as dairy cheese. However, dairy-free 'cream cheese' works fine in a dairy-free frosting. I've used this to complement the dairy-free nature of many vegetable-based cakes (which tend to use oils not butter) to make completely dairy-free *Crunchy nut carrot cakes* (see page 74). Which brings me to nuts …

NUT FREE, EGG FREE, SUGAR FREE …
Some people have the worst luck, with multiple allergies and intolerances. I'm conscious that nuts feature heavily in gluten-free baking, which is a real downer if you have a nut allergy, so I've included some recipes like *Christmas in Bakewell* (see page 184) where traditionally used almonds have been sent packing.

Egg replacer is widely available. I've not used it myself as yet, but I was recently chatting to a vegan drag queen baker in Manchester (oh, how I live) who swears by it.

'Sugar free' is a bit of a misnomer because there are naturally occurring sugars in all sorts of things, but if you're looking to reduce your intake of processed sugars, then there are some alternatives, notably coconut sugar, emerging. I've started to use this in some recipes.

Some recipes – like *Socca* (see page 38) and *Hot potatoes* (see page 124) – are little paragons of virtue that contain virtually nothing but flavour. But then I look again and see that there are mustard seeds in them, which is sadly a no-no for some people.

EQUIPMENT

You really don't need a lot of expensive equipment for baking. Yes, I know I have some fancy silicone moulds for madeleines and muffins and bundts, but these are really just for showing off a bit. Most of the time, you just need some decent tins and baking sheets. I use steel springform tins a lot for cakes (especially the 20cm (8in) round one) and I'm fond of my 20x30cm (8x12in) anodised aluminium tin, which puts a good crust on a focaccia and the *Portuguese sardine tart* (see page 132). I personally like big steel mixing bowls, with a few large wooden spoons and an electric hand-held mixer. A rolling pin that can be set to roll a specific thickness is really handy, which is more than can be said for some of my 'must have' purchases.

CHAPTER 1
FREE AT THE WEEKEND

For me, weekend baking usually means batches of bread. It's a great way of relaxing – pottering around when you have the time and filling the home with wonderful aromas. Good gluten-free bread can seem one of the trickiest things to master but it is possible, and you do have to put aside most of the things you learned about standard bread baking. Start with the soft, open-textured focaccia – it absorbs flavours well and is easy to make – then progress to the marginally trickier techniques that emulate the stretchiness and chewiness of a loaf containing gluten.

CARAMELISED GARLIC AND GOATS' CHEESE FOCACCIA

Makes a 20x30cm (8x12in) focaccia

This seems like an awful lot of garlic, but bear with it – caramelising it produces a rich, gentle flavour that's far from pungent. Two types of goats' cheese provide contrast – the hard cheese cubes stay fairly intact while the soft cheese melts into a golden crust. To bruise the peppercorns, just crush them very lightly in a pestle and mortar or with a rolling pin.

For the dough

450g gluten-free white bread flour blend

2 tsp quick yeast

1 tbsp caster sugar

about 1 tbsp chopped fresh rosemary

350ml milk

2 large egg whites

2 tsp balsamic vinegar

8 tbsp extra virgin olive oil, plus extra for greasing and drizzling

For the topping

2 whole garlic bulbs, cloves separated and peeled

1 tbsp olive oil

1 tsp balsamic vinegar

2 tsp brown sugar (any sort will be fine)

150ml water, plus extra for simmering the garlic

60g soft goats' cheese

60g hard goats' cheese, cubed

a small handful of fresh thyme (preferably lemon thyme), leaves picked off

$1/2$ tsp pink peppercorns, bruised

1 Line a 20x30cm (8x12in) non-stick baking tin (or similar) with well-oiled baking parchment.

2 In a large mixing bowl, stir together the flour, yeast, caster sugar and chopped rosemary.

3 Warm the milk (in a pan or microwave) until lukewarm, then beat in the egg whites and balsamic vinegar.

4 Pour the liquid into the dry ingredients and mix well, then add the oil and continue mixing. You should now have a very sloppy, unpromising-looking mess – more like a thick batter than a dough.

5 Spoon the batter into the prepared baking tin, level it out as best as you can, then cover it and leave it to rise in a fairly warm place for about 1 hour.

6 Meanwhile, get on with caramelising your garlic. Put the cloves in a pan of water, bring to the boil, then simmer for a couple of minutes. Drain and dry the cloves using kitchen paper.

7 Dry the pan, then add the oil and put over a medium heat. Add the garlic and fry for a couple of minutes, and then add the balsamic vinegar, brown sugar and water. Bring to the boil, then simmer until the liquid has reduced and the garlic is softened. Leave to cool a little.

8 Preheat the oven to 220°C/200°C fan/gas 7.

9 When the dough has risen, squish the garlic cloves into the surface. Smear flecks of the soft goats' cheese on top and scatter with cubes of the hard goats' cheese, the thyme leaves and pink peppercorns.

10 Drizzle generously with olive oil and bake for about 40 minutes, until risen and golden.

TAPIOCA TAPENADE COBS

Makes 12 cobs

These crusty little rolls are a great addition to a dinner party bread selection, with their tasty tapenade cores, but they're also lovely for everyday, with soup or cheese. Tailor the tapenade to taste – try capers, sundried tomatoes or anchovies along with, or in place of, the ingredients below.

For the dough
150g tapioca flour
75g gram flour
1 tsp quick yeast
a pinch of salt
grated zest of ¹/2 lemon

175ml milk (non-dairy is fine)
2 large egg whites
100g white gluten-free bread flour
   blend
3 tbsp extra virgin olive oil

For the tapenade
50g black pitted olives, drained
1 garlic clove, peeled and chopped
a small handful of fresh parsley
   (about 10g)

1 Put the tapioca flour and gram flour in a large mixing bowl. Add the yeast, salt and lemon zest and stir together.

2 Warm the milk in a small pan on the hob or in a heatproof jug in the microwave, then whisk in the egg whites. Add this to the bowl and stir to make a batter. Add the gluten-free bread flour to form a thicker dough.

3 Add the olive oil and stir this in – you don't want to incorporate all the oil – there should be a little halo of oil still visible at the edges of the dough. Cover the bowl and leave it in a fairly warm place for about 1 hour.

4 Preheat the oven to 220°C/200°C fan/gas 7.

5 Spoon generous tablespoons of the dough into a 12-hole muffin tin. (You don't need to grease the tin and please don't use paper cases or you'll find them welded to the bread when it's baked.)

6 Make the tapenade by chopping the olives, garlic and parsley, as finely as you like, and mixing them together.

7 Push a teaspoon of the tapenade into the centre of each roll with your finger – a bit like making a ring doughnut. Don't worry if some of the mix is left on top.

8 Bake for 20 minutes until golden and crusty. Cover the baked cobs with a clean tea towel, leave to cool in the tin for a few minutes, then transfer to a wire rack to finish cooling.

HOWARD'S TIP

This is one of the few gluten-free breads that just about works still warm from the oven – chewy and crusty – but you can also reheat the cooled cobs for a few minutes in a hot oven.

SPICED PUMPKIN BREAD

Makes a 900g (2lb) loaf

A lovely bread for autumn or winter that's perfect with a big bowl of soup. Allspice is a great partner for pumpkin and other types of squash, too – it's actually a dried berry, like a large peppercorn, so make sure you don't confuse it with mixed spice, which is a ground blend of different spices. The loaf's pumpkin spiral may separate from the dough a little, but what it loses in artistic regularity, it more than makes up for in taste.

For the roast pumpkin

about 400g pumpkin (or other squash), peeled, seeds removed, and cut into 3cm (1¼in) chunks

2 garlic cloves, peeled

½ tsp ground allspice or 1 tsp whole allspice berries, crushed

1–2 tbsp olive oil

For the dough

75g white teff flour

75g gluten-free oat flour, plus extra for dusting

150g gram flour

50g pumpkin seeds

25g gluten-free pinhead oats

3 tbsp psyllium husk powder

2 tsp quick yeast

a pinch of salt

375ml gluten-free oat milk

1 tbsp honey

1 tbsp olive oil, plus extra for shaping

1 Preheat the oven to 240°C/220°C fan/gas 9 and line a roasting tin with kitchen foil.

2 Put the prepared pumpkin in the roasting tin, add the garlic, allspice and a good glug of olive oil, and then toss well to coat the vegetables in the spiced oil. Roast for about 15 minutes until soft and charred, then leave to cool.

3 Put the flours, pumpkin seeds, pinhead oats, psyllium husk powder, yeast and salt in a large mixing bowl and stir to combine. Take the roasted garlic cloves and squish them into the dry ingredients.

4 Gently warm the oat milk in a small pan or in a heatproof jug in the microwave, add the honey and oil and stir until mixed, then stir this into the dry ingredients. Mix well with a wooden spoon to create a dough, then cover the bowl and leave it to rise in a fairly warm place for about an hour.

5 If you've turned the oven off, preheat it again to 240°C/220°C fan/gas 9. Line a 900g (2lb) loaf tin (about 21x11x6cm (8¼x4¼x2½in)) with non-stick baking parchment.

6 Tip the dough onto a lightly oiled surface and gently stretch it and press it out to form a rectangle about 30x23cm (12x9in). Squash the pieces of roasted pumpkin between your fingers to flatten them, then press them onto the surface of the dough. Now carefully roll up the dough from the shorter edge and lift it into the prepared tin, tucking it in to fit at the sides. Dust with a little more oat flour.

HOWARD'S TIP

Gluten-free bread needs time to firm up so allow it to cool completely before slicing.

---

7 Bake for 15 minutes, and then reduce the oven temperature to 220°C/200°C fan/gas 7 and bake for a further 25–30 minutes until crusty on top and sounding hollow when tapped underneath.

8 Cover with a clean cloth and leave to cool in the tin for a few minutes, then transfer to a wire rack and leave to cool completely.

CRUSTY OLIVE BREAD

Makes a medium baguette-style loaf

A great crusty loaf – this dough has enough substance to let you shape it long and almost baguette-like. Crushing the dried rosemary in a pestle and mortar ensures that you get the flavour without the unpleasant sensation of pine needles on the tongue.

50g teff flour

250g gram flour

50g polenta, plus extra for dusting

2 tsp quick yeast

3 tbsp psyllium husk powder

1 tbsp caster sugar

1 tsp dried rosemary, crushed

100ml milk

300ml warm water

1 tbsp extra virgin olive oil,
    plus extra for shaping

75g pitted olives (ideally ones
    marinated in garlic and herbs),
    drained

1 Put the flours, polenta, yeast, psyllium husk powder, sugar and $^1/_2$ tsp of the rosemary in a large mixing bowl and stir to combine.

2 Add the milk, warm water and olive oil and mix well, then cover and leave it to rise in a fairly warm place for about an hour.

3 Preheat the oven to 240°C/220°C fan/gas 9 and line a flat baking sheet with non-stick baking parchment.

4 Tip the dough out onto a lightly oiled surface. Press it out to form a rectangle, then scatter the olives over the surface and gently press them in. With a little oil on your hands, roll up the dough and shape it to form a longish baguette-shaped loaf, then transfer it to the baking sheet.

5 Mix the remaining $^1/_2$ tsp rosemary with a little polenta and scatter and gently rub this over the top surface of the loaf. Score the top of the loaf with a sharp knife.

6 Bake for 15 minutes, then turn the oven temperature down to 220°C/200°C fan/gas 7 and bake for a further 15–20 minutes until golden and crusty.

7 Transfer to a wire rack, cover with a clean tea towel and leave to cool completely before slicing.

ROASTED VEGETABLE PIZZA WITH A MASHED POTATO BASE

Makes one 25cm (10in) pizza

Rejecting the notion of calling this something clever, like a potizza, or even pizza masharita, I opted to simply tell it like it is. I think this base really needs salt. Try to roll it as thin as possible – aim for a diameter of 25cm (10in). If you like a crisper base, bake it for 10 minutes before topping. Use whatever firm tomatoes you like: beef tomatoes, plum tomatoes or kumatoes – a greeny-brown tomato hybrid.

For the roasted vegetables
1 red onion
1 red pepper
2 courgettes
3–4 firm tomatoes (including kumatoes, if available)
2 garlic cloves, peeled
a good glug of olive oil
freshly ground black pepper

For the base
250g cooked mashed potato
1 tbsp olive oil
110g gram flour, plus extra for rolling
1 tsp gluten-free baking powder
salt and freshly ground black pepper to taste

To finish
a few fresh basil leaves
about 125g mozzarella (optional if keeping the recipe dairy-free or vegan)

1 Heat the oven to 240°C/220°C fan/gas 9 and line a large roasting tin with kitchen foil (it just saves on the washing up).

2 Prepare the vegetables. Peel the onion, halve and quarter to form eight chunks. Slice the top off the pepper, remove the stalk, then deseed and cut into chunks about 3cm (1¼in) square. Slice the courgettes into discs about 2cm (¾in) thick. Halve the tomatoes, or leave them whole if they are small.

3 Put the vegetables and garlic in the roasting tin, add the olive oil, season with black pepper, then toss the vegetables in the oil – using your hands gets the best results.

4 Roast the vegetables for about 20 minutes – keep an eye on them – you want them just tender and charred at the edges.

5 Remove the vegetables from the oven and turn the oven temperature down to 200°C/180°C fan/gas 6. Line a baking sheet with non-stick baking parchment.

6 Mix the mashed potato with the olive oil, gram flour, baking powder, salt and pepper and the roasted garlic cloves, which will be soft enough to squidge into the mix. Roll out the potato dough on a floured surface to create a round base about 25cm (10in) in diameter.

7 Transfer the base to the prepared baking sheet, top with the roasted vegetables, sprinkle with the basil and mozzarella (if using) and bake for 20 minutes until the base is golden brown.

NOT QUITE WHITE LOAF

Makes a 450g (1lb) loaf

Sometimes you just want the simple things in life, like a nice slice or two of plain bread to have with jam or to make a crispy bacon sandwich. Even though I use so-called white teff flour, it's really a little beige, and the psyllium husk powder stops this from being a truly white loaf, hence the name. It's still pretty good.

125g cornflour, plus extra for dusting	3 tbsp psyllium husk powder	1 tbsp olive oil, plus extra for greasing
100g gluten-free oat flour, plus extra for shaping	2 tsp quick yeast	a pinch of salt
75g white teff flour	100ml milk (dairy or oat milk)	
	300ml warm water	
	1 tbsp light honey	

1 Put the flours, psyllium husk powder and quick yeast in a large mixing bowl and stir to combine.

2 Warm the milk in a small pan or a heatproof jug in a microwave until lukewarm, then add the warm water, honey, olive oil and a pinch of salt. Pour this into the dry ingredients and stir well to make a soft dough. Cover the bowl with a cloth and leave the dough to rise in a fairly warm place for about 1 hour.

3 Preheat the oven to 240°C/220°C fan/gas 9 and lightly oil a 450g (1lb) loaf tin (about 12x19x8cm ($4^1/_2$x$7^1/_2$x$3^1/_4$in)).

4 Tip the dough out onto a surface lightly dusted with oat flour and gently shape it into an oval, a little larger than the tin.

5 Lift the dough into the tin, dust it with a little cornflour, then slash the top once lengthways with a sharp knife.

6 Bake for 15 minutes, then turn the oven temperature down to 220°C/200°C fan/gas 7 and bake for a further 20–25 minutes until golden on top and hollow-sounding when tapped on the base.

7 Transfer to a wire rack, cover with a clean tea towel and leave to cool completely before slicing.

SEEDED LOAF

Makes a 15cm (6in) round loaf

This is packed with seedy goodness and it has a great granary texture. Generally, I try to use as little salt as possible but I think this is one loaf that really needs it. I usually bake this in a small round cake tin, about 15cm (6in) in diameter, but a large, clean terracotta plant pot would be fitting, or you could use a loaf tin if you prefer.

150g tapioca flour
100g teff flour
50g quinoa flour
25g quinoa flakes
50g mixed seeds (such as pumpkin, sunflower, linseed and hemp seeds), plus extra for the top

1 tsp mustard seeds (optional)
3 tbsp psyllium husk powder
2 tsp quick yeast
300ml hot water
1 tbsp honey
1 tbsp olive oil, plus extra for shaping

about 75ml milk (dairy or non-dairy, such as oat or hemp)
a large pinch of salt

1 Put the flours, quinoa flakes, mixed seeds, mustard seeds (if using), psyllium husk powder and quick yeast in a large mixing bowl and stir to combine.

2 Put the hot water in a measuring jug and add the honey and olive oil, then top this up with milk to the 400ml mark and add a large pinch of salt. Pour this into the dry ingredients and stir well. Cover the bowl with a cloth and leave the dough to rise in a fairly warm place for about 1 hour.

3 Preheat the oven to 240°C/220°C fan/gas 9 and lightly oil a 15cm (6in) round cake tin.

4 Tip the dough out onto a lightly oiled work surface and shape it into a ball, a little larger than the tin.

5 Lift the dough into the tin, slash a cross in the top with a sharp knife and sprinkle with the extra seeds.

6 Bake for 15 minutes, then turn the oven temperature down to 220°C/200°C fan/gas 7 and bake for a further 20–25 minutes until golden on top and hollow-sounding when tapped on the base.

7 Transfer to a wire rack, cover with a clean tea towel and leave to cool completely before slicing.

BLACK PEPPER AND CARAWAY BREAD

Makes a 450g (1lb) loaf

If you're hankering for a hunk of dense, chewy, rye-style bread (but can't eat rye) this should do the trick. Perfect with smoked salmon for a Swedish smörgasbord or with crumbly Cheshire for a champion cheeseboard, some of the ingredients – like black coffee and date syrup – may seem odd, but they combine to bring a dark depth and complexity to the flavour without stamping their individual presence. If you're not one to get carried away by caraway, try black onion seeds instead. Allow the loaf to cool completely before slicing and your pumpernickel patience will be rewarded.

200g tapioca flour

150g brown teff flour

3 tbsp psyllium husk powder

2 tsp quick yeast

2 tsp caraway seeds

1 tsp black peppercorns, just 'bruised' (crushed very slightly in a pestle and mortar or with a rolling pin)

300ml black coffee (made with hot water and 2 heaped tsp instant espresso powder)

1 tbsp olive oil, plus extra for shaping and glazing

1 tbsp date syrup

75ml oat milk (or regular milk if not non-dairy)

1 tsp poppy seeds, to finish

1 Put the flours, psyllium husk powder, yeast, caraway seeds and peppercorns in a large mixing bowl and stir to combine.

2 Make up the coffee in a measuring jug, add the oil and date syrup and top up with oat milk to 400ml.

3 Stir this into the dry ingredients until well mixed and the dough comes together into a ball. Cover with a clean tea towel and leave to rise at warm room temperature for about an hour.

4 Preheat the oven to 230°C/210°C fan/gas 8 and line a 450g (1lb) loaf tin with lightly oiled baking parchment.

5 On a lightly oiled surface, shape the dough and place in the prepared loaf tin.

6 Sprinkle with poppy seeds, slash the top of the loaf with a sharp knife and bake for 50 minutes until golden on top and hollow-sounding when tapped on the base.

7 Transfer to a wire rack, cover with a clean tea towel, and leave to cool completely before slicing.

HOWARD'S TIP
Cover the bread while it is cooling so that some of the residual moisture is trapped and the crust doesn't get too dry.

PINE NUT AND PEACH TEA LOAF

Makes a 450g (1lb) loaf

Saffron-scented and topped with peaches, this fruity little number is great served sliced and buttered. If you use fresh peaches, they inevitably singe after 50 minutes in a hot oven, but semi-barbecued peaches still taste good.

a pinch of saffron strands	100g rice flour	1 tbsp mild and light olive oil, plus
about 50ml boiling water	3 tbsp psyllium husk powder	extra for shaping
75g pine nuts	2 tsp quick yeast	1 large fresh peach or 3–4 tinned
100g teff flour	75g sultanas	or bottled peach halves, drained
50g gram flour	350ml milk (dairy or non-dairy)	
	1 tbsp honey	

1 Soak the saffron in the boiling water for 30 minutes.

2 Heat a heavy-based pan and toast the pine nuts over a low-medium heat until they just start to colour, shaking the pan occasionally. Quickly tip them out of the pan into a large mixing bowl. (If you leave them in the pan they will continue to scorch, even off the heat.)

3 Add the flours, psyllium husk powder, yeast and sultanas.

4 Heat the milk in a pan or in the microwave and add the saffron and its soaking water, honey and oil.

5 Stir this into the dry ingredients until well mixed and the dough comes together into a ball. Cover with a clean tea towel and leave to rise at warm room temperature for about 1 hour.

6 Preheat the oven to 220°C/200°C fan/gas 7 and line a 450g (1lb) loaf tin or a 15cm (6in) round cake tin with baking parchment.

7 When the dough has risen, tip it onto a lightly oiled work surface and shape it to fit your chosen tin.

8 If you are using a fresh peach, remove the stone and cut it into segments. If you're using tinned or bottled peaches, you can cut them into segments or leave them halved. Press the peaches, skin-side up if they are fresh, into the top of the loaf.

9 Bake for about 50 minutes until the loaf sounds hollow when tapped underneath.

10 Cover with a clean tea towel and leave to cool completely in the tin before slicing.

YORKSHIRE TEACAKES

Makes 6 teacakes

These are Yorkshire teacakes for two reasons – firstly because they were created in my Sheffield kitchen (somewhat tenuous as the same is true of all the recipes in this book) and secondly because you bake them in a Yorkshire pudding tin. I use the standard-sized tin, which has four indentations – slightly frustrating because the recipe makes six. You could invest in two tins or just leave a couple hanging around a while longer whilst you bake the first batch – they won't come to any harm.

Baking in the tin gives a lovely crust to the teacake bottom. You'll find they bake a little flatter than most teacakes, but slice them and toast them and nobody will care – they are truly delicious! Soaking the fruit first ensures it's plump and juicy – I used Earl Grey tea for a little subtle flavour but Yorkshire tea would be entirely appropriate.

25g dried cherries	1 tsp quick yeast	2 large egg whites
20g candied peel	1 tbsp caster sugar	grated zest of $1/2$ lemon
50g sultanas	a pinch of salt	1 tbsp sunflower oil, plus extra for
1 tea bag of choice	a little freshly grated nutmeg	greasing the tins
boiling water	seeds from 5 cardamom pods,	
225g gluten-free white bread flour	crushed (optional)	
blend	175ml gluten-free oat milk	

1 Put the dried cherries, candied peel and sultanas in a small bowl, pop a tea bag in with them and top up with boiling water. Leave for an hour or so, or overnight.

2 When you're ready to bake, remove the tea bag and drain off any excess liquid.

3 Put the flour, yeast, sugar, salt, grated nutmeg and crushed cardamom in a large mixing bowl and stir to combine.

4 Gently warm the oat milk in a small pan on the hob or in a heatproof jug in the microwave. Remove from the heat, add the egg whites and lemon zest and whisk them in, then pour the liquid into the dry ingredients and mix well. Add the fruit and the oil and stir this in too, mixing until the dough comes together.

5 Lightly oil two 4-hole Yorkshire pudding tins – you will only be making 6 teacakes in total. Divide the dough into 6 and spoon the mixture into the tins. Cover with a clean damp tea towel and leave the dough to prove at warm room temperature for 30 minutes.

6 Preheat the oven to 220°C/200°C fan/gas 7.

7 Bake the teacakes for 15–20 minutes until golden. Transfer to a wire rack, cover with a clean tea towel and leave to cool completely.

8 Serve sliced and lightly toasted (I think on one side only, but it's your choice).

HOWARD'S TIP
I'm not a fan of the very finely chopped mixed peel commonly sold in tubs. Look out for whole candied peel that you can snip into larger strands and chunks.

TWO-POTATO FARLS

Makes 4 farls

Who needs a lesson in maths before breakfast? Just to say that *farl* is a Gaelic word meaning four parts, which is why the dough of a farl is traditionally quartered. With both sweet and standard potatoes this should be a simple exercise in short division – two divided by four. Oh, but should this really be three-potato, as there's potato flour in there too?
If you are clever, you will roll the potato dough to a size comfortably accommodated by your pan. If, like me, you have a tendency to regularly miss the signs for common sense, you'll have to cook two farls at a time.

2 medium-sized potatoes (about 400g in total), peeled and cut into 3–4cm (1^1/4–1^1/2in) chunks
1 medium-sized sweet potato (about 200g), peeled and cut into 3–4cm (1^1/4–1^1/2in) chunks

2 tsp chopped chives
^{1}/2 tsp caraway seeds (optional)
50g potato flour
50g gluten-free oat flour, plus extra for rolling

1 tbsp olive oil
salt and freshly ground black pepper

1 Put the potato and sweet potato chunks in a large pan of cold water. Bring to the boil, cover the pan and simmer over a medium-high heat until just tender – no more than 10 minutes. Do not overcook, as they will go watery.

2 Mash them and leave them to cool, then add the chives, caraway seeds (if using), potato flour, oat flour and olive oil. Season with salt and pepper and mix well with a wooden spoon.

3 Tip the dough onto a lightly floured surface and add a little more flour on top of the dough. Roll it out into a circle just smaller than the non-stick frying pan you intend to cook it in – ideally at least 28cm (11^1/4in) – then cut the circle into quarters.

4 Heat the frying pan over a medium heat, then add the farls and cook for about 5–7 minutes on each side until golden and crusted. If you haven't planned ahead and can't fit all four in the pan at once (see note above), keep the first pair warm in the oven while you cook the other two.

> **HOWARD'S TIP**
> Serve the farls with butter, scrambled eggs or grilled tomatoes, or as part of a full English breakfast.

PESHWARI FLATBREADS

Makes 4–6 flatbreads

I hesitate to call these naan but they serve the same purpose. The fragrant dough and sweet, nutty topping make a great partner to a good curry. They are easy to make, although the soft dough needs careful handling so work with lightly oiled hands.

For the dough
175g gluten-free white bread flour blend
50g gram flour
1 tsp quick yeast
a pinch of salt
1 tbsp caster sugar
seeds from 4–5 cardamom pods, crushed

$^1/_2$ tsp black onion seeds
175ml non-dairy milk (such as almond or coconut)
2 large egg whites
3 tbsp sunflower oil, plus extra for shaping

For the topping
35g pistachios
35g sultanas

1 Put the flours, yeast, salt, sugar, crushed cardamom seeds and onion seeds In a large mixing bowl and stir to combine.

2 Gently warm the non-dairy milk in a small pan on the hob or in a heatproof jug in the microwave. Add the egg whites and whisk them in, then pour the liquid into the dry ingredients and mix well. Add the oil and stir this in too until the dough comes together in a ball.

3 Cover the bowl with a clean tea towel and leave the dough to rise at warm room temperature for about 1 hour.

4 Make the topping by whizzing the pistachios and sultanas together in a nut grinder or food processor.

5 Line a baking sheet with baking parchment.

6 When the dough has risen, lightly oil your hands. Take a small handful of dough and gently shape it into an oval. Place this on the lined baking sheet and flatten – it should be about 10cm (4in) long. Repeat this with the rest of the dough, oiling your hands again, if necessary, until you have 4–6 flatbreads.

7 Sprinkle the topping on the flatbreads, then cover with a clean damp cloth and let them rest for about 20 minutes before baking.

8 Preheat the oven to 220°C/200°C fan/gas 7 and bake the flatbreads for 10–12 minutes until golden brown.

9 Transfer to a wire rack to cool slightly before serving.

> **HOWARD'S TIP**
> You can reheat the flatbreads by sprinkling with a little water and popping them into a hot oven or under the grill for a few minutes.

GREEK FLATBREADS

Makes 4–6 flatbreads

Like the Peshwari flatbreads, these are naan-ish, but here the gyros seasoning (usually used to flavour kebab meat) gives them a definite Greek flavour – Naan à Mouskouri perhaps?

175g gluten-free white bread flour blend

50g polenta

1 tsp quick yeast

a pinch of salt

175ml milk

2 large egg whites

1 tbsp honey

3 tbsp extra virgin olive oil, plus extra for shaping

2 tsp gyros seasoning (I use The Spice Shop's)

125g halloumi cheese, cubed

a few black olives, pitted and quartered

2 tsp sesame seeds

1 Put the flour, polenta, yeast and salt in a large mixing bowl and stir to combine.

2 Gently warm the milk in a small pan on the hob or in a heatproof jug in the microwave. Add the egg whites and whisk them in, along with the honey, then pour the liquid into the dry ingredients and mix well. Add the oil and gyros seasoning and stir them in too.

3 Cover the bowl with a clean tea towel and leave the dough to rise at warm room temperature for about 1 hour.

4 Line a baking sheet with baking parchment.

5 When the dough has risen, rub your hands with a little oil, take a small handful of dough and gently shape it into a circle or oval. Place this on the lined baking sheet and flatten. Repeat this with the rest of the dough, oiling your hands again if necessary, until you have 4–6 flatbreads.

6 Press the halloumi into the surface of the flatbreads and press pieces of olive in between, sprinkle with sesame seeds, then cover the flatbreads with a clean damp cloth and let them rest for about 20 minutes.

7 Preheat the oven to 220°C/200°C fan/gas 7.

8 Bake the flatbreads for about 15 minutes until firm and golden and the halloumi is charred. Transfer to a wire rack to cool.

SOCCA

Makes two 20x30cm (8x12in) socca

Part flatbread, part pancake, this French Provençal street food is a traditional use of gram, or chickpea, flour. Normally served as an appetiser, I make it a little more substantial with the addition of whole chickpeas and give a nod to this Moroccan influence with lemon thyme and *ras el hanout* spices. Moorish and moreish, it's best served immediately, but you can keep any leftover batter in the fridge for later.

150g gram flour	1 tbsp olive oil, plus extra for
500ml water	cooking
a pinch of Maldon or Fleur de Sel	about 120g cooked chickpeas (half
salt	a can, drained and dried with
about 1 tsp fresh lemon thyme	kitchen paper)
leaves	1 tsp ras el hanout spice blend

1 Whisk together the gram flour, water, salt, thyme leaves and 1 tbsp oil until smooth with no lumps. The easiest way to do this is with an electric stick blender. Cover the batter and leave for about 2 hours.

2 Toss the chickpeas in the ras el hanout spices.

3 Either preheat the grill to high or preheat the oven to its highest setting. Put about 2 tbsp olive oil in a non-stick baking tin. (I use an anodised aluminium one that's 20x30cm (8x12in), but you could use a round one.) Heat this under the grill or in the oven until the oil is smoking hot.

4 Pour about half the batter mix into the tin to cover the base and scatter on half the chickpeas. Cook for about 5 minutes until charred. Then remove the socca to a plate and repeat with the remaining batter.

5 Cut with a knife or pizza wheel and serve hot.

DUTCH DOUGHNUTS

Makes 20 doughnuts

This is my gluten-free and dairy-free take on the traditional Dutch doughnut called *oliebollen*, or oily balls. Now, if the thought of that hasn't put you off, then you're in for a treat. Best eaten fresh, as soon as they're cool enough to handle, this is a ball game with no keepers, so halve the quantities if you're not baking for both sides.

For the dough
450g white gluten-free bread flour
2 tsp quick yeast
3 tbsp muscovado sugar
a pinch of salt
350ml almond milk (or other non-dairy milk)

1 tsp lemon juice
2 large eggs
1 tsp vanilla paste (or equivalent of vanilla extract)
3 tbsp mild and light olive oil
75g raisins
50g dried pear or dried apple

For frying and finishing
sunflower oil, for frying
cornflour, for shaping
vanilla dusting sugar, to finish

1 Put the flour, yeast, muscovado sugar and salt in a large mixing bowl and stir to combine.

2 Heat the almond milk in a pan, or in a heatproof jug in the microwave until warm, then add the lemon juice and beat in the eggs and vanilla.

3 Pour the liquid into the dry ingredients, stir with a wooden spoon until combined, then add the olive oil and stir again. Cover the bowl and leave the dough to rise at warm room temperature for an hour or so.

4 When the dough has risen, add the dried fruit and stir gently, trying not to deflate the dough. Cover again and leave while you heat the oil for frying.

5 Pour sunflower oil into a very large, heavy-based pan or deep-fat fryer to a depth of at least 5cm (2in). Heat the oil to 150–160°C. If you are doing this on the hob, you will need to use a thermometer and keep watching – have the ring on a medium heat and turn it up or down as needed.

6 Dust your hands with cornflour to avoid the dough sticking, then take a generous tablespoon of dough and gently roll it into a ball, then drop this into the hot oil. It will sink, then bob up to the top as it cooks. The doughnuts will take about 5 minutes to cook.

7 Repeat with more dough, frying in manageable batches. If the odd bit of fruit escapes, just fish it out with a strainer. When the dough balls are golden all over, take them out with the strainer and drain on kitchen paper. Dust with vanilla sugar before serving warm.

> **HOWARD'S TIP**
> You can buy ready-made vanilla dusting sugar, which is powdery (like icing sugar) or make your own vanilla sugar by leaving a couple of vanilla pods in a small jar of caster sugar. You can use the pods once you've scraped out the seeds into another recipe, such as a custard.

CHAPTER 2

FREE IN THE WEEK

With less time to spare, it's good to have a stock of supper-time staples and tea-time treats to draw upon. I'm not saying these are all the quickest things to prepare, but I often find it's good to get home from work and 'switch off' with some fairly undemanding baking. At other times, you'll thank goodness there's emergency sustenance in the cake tin.

PESTO PASTIES

Makes 4–6 pasties, depending on size

Hearty lunch box packers, these pesto-inspired pasties are never going to win awards for their Latin looks. More like Italian builders – a little rough around the edges and with a tendency to exposed cracks – their redeeming feature is that they taste *bello*.

For the filling
- 2 smallish potatoes (about 250–300g in total), peeled and cut into 1cm (¹/₂in) chunks
- 1 tbsp olive oil
- 1 small red onion, finely chopped
- 50g pine nuts
- a large handful of fresh basil leaves (the whole of a supermarket medium-sized basil pot or equivalent)
- 100g firm white cheese (ideally *ricotta salata dura* or a hard goats' cheese), grated
- freshly ground black pepper

For the pastry
- 150g wholegrain brown rice flour, plus extra for rolling
- 50g millet flour
- 50g potato flour
- 50g gluten-free pinhead oats
- ¹/₄ tsp gluten-free baking powder
- 100g cold unsalted butter, cubed
- 30g fresh Parmesan cheese, grated
- 2 garlic cloves, peeled and crushed, grated or finely chopped
- 1 large egg
- 1 large egg white (save the yolk for glazing)
- 1 tsp cold water (optional)

To finish
- 1 egg yolk

1 Put the potatoes in a pan of cold water, bring to the boil and simmer for 5 minutes or so, until tender but still intact. Drain and leave to cool a little.

2 Heat the oil in a large frying pan, wok or sauté pan and fry the onion gently until soft. Add the pine nuts and fry these gently too. Add the cooked potatoes to the pan and stir to coat them in the oil.

3 Turn off the heat and add the basil and cheese. Season with black pepper but don't add salt, as the cheeses in the filling and pastry are salty enough. Leave to one side while you prepare the pastry.

4 Preheat the oven to 180°C/160°C fan/gas 4 and line a baking sheet with baking parchment.

5 To make the pastry, put the flours, oats and baking powder in a large mixing bowl and stir together to combine. Add the butter and rub through until there are no lumps visible, then stir in the Parmesan and garlic.

6 Whisk the egg and egg white and add this to the flour mix. Stir through with a knife, and then bring the dough together with your hands. Adding a little water at this stage will produce a finished crust that is slightly less crumbly and crack-prone, but a little harder – it's your choice.

7 On a floured surface, roll half the dough out to about 5mm (¼in) thick. (My pre-set rolling pin has a choice of 4mm or 6mm – I go for the latter, which means fewer or smaller pasties and some leftover filling).

8 Cut a circle of pastry using a saucer or small side plate as a template. Transfer this to the baking sheet. Spoon some of the filling in the middle (if you want the classic stegosaurus-backed pasties) or on one half (for the flatter, semi-circle shape). Brush the pastry edge with beaten egg yolk, press together to seal and crimp by hand or indent with the prongs of a fork.

9 Transfer the pasties to the baking sheet and bake for 40–45 minutes until golden brown. Serve warm or cold.

> **HOWARD'S TIP**
> Any leftover filling makes a great Spanish omelette – albeit an Italianesque one.

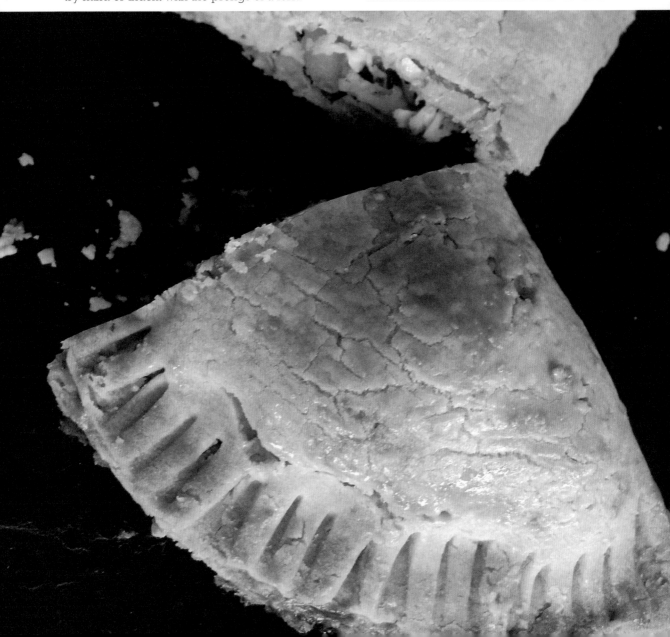

CHICKEN POT PIE WITH TARRAGON TOP CRUST

Serves 4–6

If *coq au vin* is chicken in a van, this one has herbs in the roof rack. It has a very short, crumbly pastry lid – if you prefer a firmer pastry, try adding a spot or two of guar gum and a little more water. For a meaty alternative, the pastry in the Chorizo straws (see page 112) is good on top too.

For the pastry

180g gluten-free white bread flour blend

20g gram flour, plus extra for rolling

100g cold unsalted butter (or dairy-free olive oil spread), cubed

1 large egg, beaten

2 tbsp ice cold water

a handful of fresh tarragon leaves

For the pie filling

2 tbsp olive oil

3 echalion shallots (or about 6 ordinary shallots), peeled and sliced about 1cm (½in) thick

6 free-range skinless and boneless chicken thigh fillets (about 550g)

1 garlic clove, peeled and thinly sliced

1 tsp pink peppercorns

350g assorted mushrooms (such as 100g girolle mushrooms and 250g chestnut mushrooms)

1 tbsp gram flour

150ml white wine

1 chicken stock cube (I use Kallo very low salt organic chicken)

1 To make the pastry, put the flours in a large bowl and stir together to combine, then rub in the butter to breadcrumb consistency.

2 Using a knife, stir in most of the beaten egg (you can save a little for glazing the crust). Add 1–2 tbsp ice cold water and bring the mix together, using your hand, to form a soft dough. Wrap in cling film and chill in the fridge for about 30 minutes while you cook the chicken.

3 Preheat the oven to 200°C/180°C fan/gas 6.

4 To make the pie filling, heat the oil in a sauté pan or wok and fry the shallots over a medium heat for 2 minutes.

5 Add the chicken thighs, brown them on one side for 5 minutes, then turn them over and brown on the other side too.

6 After another 2 minutes, add the garlic and peppercorns. Make sure the inner surfaces of the chicken are cooking too – spread out and divide the thighs in half if necessary.

7 Add the mushrooms and gram flour and stir, then add the wine and stock cube and simmer for 5 minutes while you roll out the pastry.

8 On a lightly floured surface, roll out the pastry a little, then scatter with tarragon leaves and continue to roll out so they are pressed into the pastry.

9 Transfer the pie filling to an ovenproof pie dish (I use an oval dish about 25x19cm (10x7½in) but a similar-size round or rectangular one is fine too), and then top with the tarragon pastry. Crimp the edge and decorate with spare pastry if you wish. Brush with the leftover beaten egg and bake for 40–45 minutes until golden brown.

HOWARD'S TIP

Echalion shallots – also called banana shallots – are worth looking out for. A cross between a shallot and an onion, they are larger and longer than ordinary shallots. Elegant when whole, echalions also slice and chop easily when a recipe cries out for a very finely chopped onion. They are also a darn sight easier to peel than your standard shallots.

SPRING VEGETABLE TARTLETS

Makes at least eight 9cm (3^1/$_2$in) tartlets

Baby vegetables need hardly any cooking at all. Here they're quickly blanched, then tossed in a minty, lemony, garlicky dressing. Poppy seeds and pinhead oats add crunchy contrast in cute little quiche tins.

For the pastry

150g wholegrain rice flour, plus extra for rolling

50g quinoa flour

50g cornflour

50g gluten-free pinhead oats

^{1}/$_4$ tsp gluten-free baking powder

100g cold unsalted butter, cubed, plus extra for greasing the tins

25–30g Parmesan or pecorino cheese

freshly ground black pepper

2 tsp poppy seeds

1 large egg

1 large egg white (save the yolk for the filling)

For the filling

about 200g baby vegetables, such as fine beans, asparagus or baby carrots

1 tbsp olive oil

2 spring onions, finely sliced

1 garlic clove, peeled and crushed or grated

grated zest of ^{1}/$_2$ lemon

a small handful of fresh mint leaves, finely chopped

2 large eggs

1 large egg yolk

200ml milk

75g Cheddar cheese

freshly ground black pepper

1 Mix the flours, oats and baking powder together in a large mixing bowl. Rub in the butter until it resembles breadcrumbs. Stir in the cheese, black pepper and poppy seeds.

2 Lightly whisk the egg and egg white in a bowl, pour this into the flour mix, stir with a knife, and then bring the dough together by hand.

3 Lightly grease at least eight 9cm (3^1/$_2$in) mini fluted quiche tins with loose bottoms – this is particularly important if the tins are new.

4 On a lightly floured surface, roll out half the dough to a thickness of 4mm (about ^{1}/$_4$in). I find the easiest way to line the tins is to stamp out circles using an 11cm (4^1/$_4$in) round cutter. Gently ease the discs into the tins, pressing down from the edge and working round until all is safely gathered in. Patch any cracks with pellets of pastry, and then pop the pastry cases into the freezer for 20 minutes. Repeat the process with the remaining dough.

5 Preheat the oven to 210°C/190°C fan/gas 6–7 and put a baking sheet in to heat up.

6 Put a paper muffin case inside each pastry case, fill with baking beans and bake blind for 12 minutes, then remove the baking beans and paper cases and bake for another 5 minutes to dry off the inner surface.

7 Remove the pastry cases from the oven and leave them to cool (still in their tins) while you prepare the filling. Turn the oven down to 190°C/170°C fan/gas 5.

8 Blanch the vegetables by cooking briefly in a pan of boiling water (fine beans need 30 seconds, asparagus and baby carrots take 1 minute), then drain and plunge into a bowl of cold water to stop them cooking further.

9 Heat the oil in a wok or large frying pan and gently fry the spring onions over a low to medium heat for a minute or so, then add the garlic, lemon and mint and stir together.

10 Drain the vegetables, then toss them in the warm onion dressing. Divide the vegetables between the pastry cases, making sure you share out the onion dressing too. You can try to be artistic with your vegetable arrangement but frankly your efforts may be in vain – the savoury custard will soon mask any bean sunbursts and asparagus clusters.

11 Make the custard by whisking together the eggs, egg yolk, milk, cheese and black pepper. It's best to do this in a jug so you can easily pour it into the pastry cases. Fill the cases, and then return the tray of quiches to the oven and bake for about 15 minutes until firm and golden. Cool on a wire rack before removing from the tins.

ONION AND SHALLOT TARTE TATIN

Makes a 25cm (10in) tart

A savoury take on this timeless tarte, with a classic combination of cheese and onion. Juxtapose elongated echalions with round reds for colour contrast and a little allium artistry.

For the filling

25g unsalted butter

1 tbsp olive oil

1 tsp caster sugar

3 smallish red onions (about 220g in total), peeled and halved

5 echalion shallots (about 220g in total), peeled and halved

For the pastry

75g gluten-free oat flour, plus extra for rolling

50g gram flour

25g polenta

50g cold unsalted butter, cubed

25g mature cheese, grated

$\frac{1}{2}$ tsp dried garlic granules

$\frac{1}{2}$ tsp dried rosemary, crushed

1 large egg, beaten

To serve

150g soft goats' cheese, Camembert or Brie (optional)

1 Heat the butter and oil in a large non-stick ovenproof frying pan, over a low-medium heat. When the butter has melted, add the sugar, stir to dissolve it, then place the halved red onions in the pan, cut-side down and arrange the shallots around them. Cook for about 10 minutes.

2 Turn the heat down to low, cover the pan and cook for another 10–15 minutes until the onions are cooked through but still firm. A knife should go all the way through without much resistance. If one onion is holding up progress (probably because it was a bit bigger), you can carefully lift off its outer layer. Take the pan off the heat and leave to cool.

3 Preheat the oven to 200°C/180°C fan/gas 6.

4 Put the flours and polenta in a large mixing bowl and rub in the butter until there are no lumps visible. Stir in the cheese, garlic granules and rosemary. Stir in the egg with a knife, then bring the dough together with your hands.

5 On a floured work surface, roll out the pastry into a circle slightly larger than your pan. Place the pastry circle on top of the onions and tuck the edges in.

6 Bake for about 25 minutes until the pastry is crisp and golden.

7 Leave it in the pan for a few minutes, then hold a plate against the pastry and tip the pan over to release the tart. If any onions or shallots have stuck to the pan, pick them off and return them to their rightful place on the pastry.

8 If you like, you can now dot little pieces of cheese between the onions and pop it back in the oven to melt. Just make sure you use an ovenproof plate.

RED VEGETABLE AND BEAN COBBLER

Serves 4

There's a lot of red going on here – red onions, red pepper, red kidney beans … red wine! Using tinned beans in chilli sauce adds body and a gentle little kick to the casserole, but always double check that the thickeners used are gluten free. You can easily make this dairy free, using a non-dairy milk and olive oil spread in the scone mix. If dairy isn't a problem, then a little cheese on top wouldn't go amiss. For consistency in the colour palette, it may have to be Red Leicester!

For the casserole

1 tbsp oil

2 small red onions, roughly chopped

2 garlic cloves, peeled and finely chopped or sliced

1 red pepper, deseeded and roughly chopped

1 large carrot, cut into 1cm (^{1}/2in) chunks

100ml red wine or water

1 vegetable stock cube

1 tsp fresh thyme leaves or ^{1}/2 tsp dried thyme

250g mushrooms, sliced, quartered or left whole, depending on size

400g tin of chopped tomatoes

400g tin of red kidney beans in chilli sauce

For the scone mix

200g rice flour, plus extra for rolling

50g gram flour

1 tsp xanthan gum

4 tsp gluten-free baking powder

^{1}/2 tsp smoked paprika

50g unsalted butter (or dairy-free olive oil spread)

3–4 sundried tomatoes in oil, drained and finely chopped or snipped

250ml milk (use gluten-free oat milk if baking non-dairy)

about 20g Red Leicester cheese (optional)

1 Heat the oil in a large frying pan or wok and gently fry the onion and garlic over a low heat until softened.

2 Add the red pepper and carrot and turn up the heat a little to medium. Cover and allow the vegetables to sweat for 2 minutes.

3 Add the red wine or water and simmer for a further 2 minutes. Add the stock cube and let this dissolve, then add the fresh or dried thyme. Add the mushrooms, tomatoes and beans. Cover and turn off the heat.

4 Pre-heat the oven to 220°C/200°C fan/gas 7.

5 Transfer the vegetable and bean mixture to an ovenproof dish (a large shallow casserole dish, deep lasagne dish or the bottom half of a tagine would all work).

6 Begin to make the scone mix by mixing the flours, xanthan gum, baking powder and paprika. Rub in the butter, or spread, to breadcrumb consistency. Add the chopped sundried tomatoes, and then stir in the milk to form a very soft dough.

7 On a lightly floured surface, roll or pat the dough into a circle about 2.5cm (1in) thick. Cut out circles about 6cm (2½in) in diameter and place on top of the vegetables.

8 Scatter with cheese (if using) and bake for 20 minutes until golden. Serve hot.

HERBY YORKSHIRE PUDDING

Serves 4–6

When my sister and I were little, my mum used to ring the changes with a variation on the classic Yorkshire pudding, which she called season pudding (as in Yorkshire pudding with seasoning). Essentially this consisted of grating in a white onion and adding some dried mixed herbs to the batter. Tasty though it was, I remember it sometimes produced a slightly wet pudding as the moist raw onion seeped a little, rather than cooking through properly. (What a precocious child I must have been – never a fussy eater but a food critic from an early age!) This gluten-free and dairy-free version makes use of the wider choice of seasonings around nowadays, with fresh chives and finely chopped sundried tomatoes.

2 tbsp rice bran oil	100g tapioca flour	a handful of fresh chives, chopped
4 large eggs	50g gluten-free oat flour	or snipped
300ml gluten-free oat milk	50g gram flour	about 6 sundried tomatoes in oil,
a pinch of salt	50g cornflour	drained and chopped
freshly milled black pepper	1/2 tsp gluten-free baking powder	

1 Preheat the oven to 240°C/220°C fan/gas 9. Put the oil in a metal baking tin about 20x30cm (8x12in) and heat this in the oven.

2 Whisk the eggs with the milk and add the salt and pepper.

3 Whisk in the flours and baking powder, and then add the chives and tomatoes.

4 When the oil is smoking hot, pour in the batter and bake for 20 minutes until risen and golden brown.

> **HOWARD'S TIP**
> Rice bran oil is great for coking at high temperatures as it has a high smoke point. Extracted from the brown outer layer of rice grains, it has a light taste and contains no cholesterol.

FRESH BLACKBERRY AND ALMOND SCONES

Makes 6–8 scones

It's no surprise to find a bit of fruit in our scones – the odd raisin, maybe even a glacé cherry or two. But would you really consider fresh fruit, with its dangerous tendencies to ooze and dribble? Why it could even turn into jam, and whoever heard of scones and … I rest my case. The blackberries do indeed splurt and seep a little erratically but personally I find the random ripple rather attractive. Sugar comes only from the berries and the almond milk, but you could add a spoonful in the mix or sprinkle a little Demerara on top if you have a sweeter tooth. Replace the butter with a sunflower spread if you need these to be dairy free – if not, serve with clotted cream or mascarpone.

150g rice flour, plus extra for shaping

50g millet flour

50g ground almonds

2 tsp xanthan gum

4 tsp gluten-free baking powder

50g cold unsalted butter, cubed (or dairy-free sunflower spread)

75g fresh blackberries, washed and patted dry with kitchen paper

180–200ml almond milk drink

a few drops of almond extract

a little beaten egg for glazing (optional)

1 Preheat the oven to 220°C/200°C fan/gas 7 and line a baking sheet with baking parchment.

2 Mix the flours, ground almonds, xanthan gum and baking powder in a large bowl. Rub in the butter (or sunflower spread) until there are no lumps visible.

3 Cut the blackberries in half (or quarters, if very large), add them to the bowl and gently toss to coat them in the flour mix.

4 Add the 180ml of the almond milk and the almond extract and stir with a wooden spoon. Depending on the juiciness of the fruit, you may need to add the remaining almond milk but it should be a very soft dough.

5 Tip the dough onto a well-floured surface, and pat it down gently (dust with a little more flour on top if necessary) to a thickness of about 2.5cm (1in).

6 Cut out the scones using a 6cm (1½in) round cutter and carefully transfer them to the baking sheet. Gather together any spare dough, clump it together and pat it down again to cut more scones. The more you handle it, the more the fruit will squelch, so try to be as gentle as you can.

7 Brush the top surface of the scones with beaten egg (if using) and bake for 15–20 minutes until risen and golden. Transfer to a wire rack to cool.

THAI TEA TRAYBAKE

Makes a 23cm (9in) square traybake that cuts into 25 pieces

Ginger, coconut, lemongrass and lime make a lovely moist traybake that brings Thai tea to high tea.

For the lemongrass syrup
2 lemongrass stalks, roughly sliced
juice of 1 lime (use the zest in the cake)
about 75ml hot water
100g caster sugar

For the cake
150g butter (or dairy-free spread)
150g caster sugar
grated zest of 1 lime
2 pieces of preserved stem ginger in syrup, drained and finely chopped
125g rice flour
1 tsp xanthan gum
2 tsp gluten-free baking powder
3 large eggs
50g desiccated coconut

To decorate
4–5 pieces of preserved stem ginger in syrup, drained and thinly sliced into 25 slices (about 60–80g)

1 To make the lemongrass syrup, put the lemongrass and lime juice in a measuring jug and top up with hot water to the 100ml mark. Add the caster sugar. Heat in the microwave (or pour it into a small pan and heat) until the sugar has dissolved. Leave to cool, then cover and keep in the fridge until needed, ideally overnight.

2 Preheat the oven to 180°C/160°C fan/gas 4. Lightly grease a 23cm (9in) square baking tin and line it with baking parchment.

3 In a large mixing bowl, cream the butter with the sugar and lime zest, using an electric hand-held mixer or wooden spoon, until light and fluffy. Stir in the finely chopped preserved stem ginger.

4 In a separate bowl, sift the rice flour with the xanthan gum and baking powder. Add a spoonful of this and 1 egg to the butter and sugar mixture and beat it in thoroughly. Add the rest of the eggs, one by one, adding a spoonful of the flour mixture each time. Fold in the rest of the flour, then fold in the desiccated coconut.

5 Spoon the mixture into the prepared tin and bake for about 25 minutes until firm and golden.

6 While the cake is in the oven, pour the syrup through a small sieve or tea strainer to remove the pieces of lemongrass. (If the syrup has been in the fridge, you can warm it up again to make it more liquid.) With a teaspoon, press firmly against the lemongrass in the sieve to ensure you squeeze out every last drop of its flavour and aroma.

7 As soon as the cake comes out of the oven, douse it liberally with the lemongrass syrup, then leave it to cool in the tin, topping it up with more lemongrass syrup and letting the cake absorb it.

8 When the cake is cool, take it out of the tin, decorate it evenly with the 25 slices of stem ginger, then cut it into 25 pieces so each one has a slice of ginger.

AMSTERDAM APPLE CAKE

Makes a 20cm (8in) cake

A pistachio-topped apple pie I once ate in Amsterdam inspired this aromatic cake.
I remember being very impressed by the combination of flavours, and by the steel siphons
filled with real double cream to pump on top (none of that sad squirty fake cream nonsense).
Hemp flour adds flavour (and an appropriate talking point), but replace it if it's not your
scene, man. It's great served Amsterdam-style with cream, but it also makes a comforting pud
served warm with custard.

For the streusel topping
25g cold unsalted butter, cubed
50g rice flour
50g Demerara sugar
25g chopped pistachios

For the cake
175g unsalted butter
175g light soft brown sugar
50g rice flour
50g potato flour
25g hemp flour (optional – replace with more rice and potato flour if you prefer)
2 tsp gluten-free baking powder
1 tsp xanthan gum
1 tsp ground cinnamon
3 large eggs
50g roasted chopped hazelnuts
75g sultanas
about 200g apples (preferably Cox or Granny Smith)

1 Preheat the oven to 190°C/170°C fan/gas 5. Lightly butter a 20cm (8in) springform tin and line it with baking parchment.

2 Make the streusel topping in a bowl by rubbing the butter into the rice flour until it's like lumpy sand, then stir in the Demerara sugar and chopped pistachios.

3 In a large mixing bowl, make the cake by creaming the butter and soft brown sugar together.

4 In a separate bowl, sift together the rice, potato and hemp flours, with the baking powder, xanthan gum and cinnamon.

5 Add a spoonful of the flour mixture and one egg to the butter and sugar mixture, beating it in thoroughly. Add the rest of the eggs, one by one, adding a spoonful of the flour mixture each time. Fold in the rest of the flour, and then fold in the chopped hazelnuts and sultanas. Spoon the mixture into the prepared tin and level the top.

6 Peel and core the apples and slice them horizontally, then cut the apple rings in half. Place the apple slices on top of the cake mix, overlapping as necessary. If you arrange it so you have an apple ring (or two halves) with a hole in the very centre of the cake, you'll be able to test the cake is done without squelching through apple flesh.

7 Scatter the streusel topping over the apple and bake for at least 1 hour until a cake tester inserted in the centre of the cake comes out clean. Leave to cool slightly, then remove from the tin and cool on a wire rack.

BLUE LAVENDER AND AMARANTH CAKE

Makes a 26cm (10^1/$_2$in) cake

Imagine a blueberry upside-down cake encountering a lemon drizzle cake in a summer flower garden. Amid knowingly nodding spears of amaranth and a whispering breeze of lavender a *liaison délicieux* occurs. Nine months later, Bob's your uncle, Fanny's your aunt – the encounter bears fruit and this cake is born. Fortunately, in reality, it only takes around an hour to reproduce. Amaranth flakes provide a lovely texture – light but dense, if that's not a culinary contradiction. The lavender and lemon syrup really is very subtle – add a little more lavender if you like more than a romantic whisper.

For the cake
200g dairy-free sunflower spread (or unsalted butter)
200g caster sugar
grated zest of 2 lemons (use the juice for the syrup)
100g amaranth flakes
100g pistachios, coarsely ground or finely chopped
100g cornflour
1^1/$_2$ tsp gluten-free baking powder
3 large eggs
200g fresh blueberries, washed and dried

For the syrup
juice of 2 lemons
75g icing sugar
^{1}/$_2$ tsp dried lavender (add more if you prefer a stronger lavender flavour)

1 Pre-heat the oven to 180°C/160°C fan/gas 4 and line a 26cm (10^1/$_2$in) springform cake tin with non-stick baking parchment.

2 In a large mixing bowl, cream the sunflower spread (or butter) and sugar together with the lemon zest until pale and light.

3 In a separate bowl, combine the amaranth flakes, pistachios, cornflour and baking powder, then add a little of this into the butter and sugar mix, followed by an egg. Mix well, alternating the dry ingredients with an egg, until it's all combined.

4 Scatter the blueberries over the base of the prepared tin, then spoon the cake mixture on top and level it out.

5 Bake for about 45–50 minutes until firm to the touch and beginning to shrink from the sides.

6 Meanwhile, to make the syrup, mix the lemon juice with the icing sugar and lavender. Heat in a small pan (or give it a blast in the microwave in a suitable jug) until the sugar has dissolved.

7 Allow the cake to cool in its tin. While the cake is still warm, pour some of the syrup over it, then keep topping up until you have used up all the syrup or the cake looks as if it can't take any more.

8 When ready to serve, un-spring the tin, upturn the cake onto a plate or cake stand and carefully remove the baking parchment.

GREENGAGE SUMMER PAVLOVA

Serves 4

A favourite childhood film of mine and my sister, *The Greengage Summer*, tells a story of fragile loyalties and innocence lost. Interpreting this classic through the medium of pudding (yes, my tongue is firmly in my cheek), I came up with fragile meringue and booze-sullied fruit. Like summer and childhood, the greengage season is short, so use other plums if they're not available. The meringue includes manuka honey – a nod to the Pavlova's antipodean origins – but any good honey will do if you're not picky about cultural authenticity on your dessert plate. Sipsmith's Summer Cup has elements of Earl Grey tea and limoncello, so you could make a summer marinade from those ingredients if you can't find it.

For the meringue
4 large egg whites
^{1}/4 tsp cream of tartar
220g caster sugar
2 tbsp manuka honey (or other honey of choice)

a few drops of rosewater
1 tsp white wine vinegar
2 tsp cornflour
about 25g pistachios, roughly chopped

For the topping
about 400g greengages (or other ripe plums)
about 75ml Sipsmith's Summer Cup
double cream or whipping cream

1 Preheat the oven to 140°C/120°C fan/gas 1 and line a baking sheet with baking parchment.

2 In a large mixing bowl, using an electric hand-held mixer, whisk the egg whites and cream of tartar to soft peaks. Add the sugar, a little at a time, whisking continuously, until the mixture is stiff and glossy.

3 Add the honey, rosewater and vinegar and whisk them in, then sift in the cornflour and gently fold this in with a metal spoon.

4 Spoon the meringue onto the lined baking tray in a circle about 24cm (9^1/2in) in diameter. Scatter the chopped pistachios on top and bake for 2^1/2 hours until firm and light golden brown on top (it will still be a little softly chewy inside). Leave it to cool on the baking parchment, then peel off and store the Pavlova in an airtight tin. (It's the nature of Pavlovas to crack a little on cooling so don't be alarmed.)

5 Halve the greengages and remove their stones, then sit them in a shallow dish or tub and pour over the Sipsmith's. Cover and let them soak up the booze for a few hours or overnight. What they lose in greenness they will gain in spirit.

6 To serve, drain the greengages but keep their marinade. Whip the cream with a little of the marinade and spread on top of the Pavlova, then top with the greengages and serve straight away.

HOWARD'S TIP
Egg whites whisk better if they're not fridge-cold. If you are taking them from the fridge, just warm them up under the hot tap for a few seconds before using.

SUNNY HONEY BUNDT

Makes a 26cm (10¹/₂in) cake

Golden mango, oranges and yellow polenta provide the sunshine for this honey bun, topped with a handful of sunflower seeds for good measure. Like most bundt cakes – which are baked in a fancy mould with a hole in the centre – this is quite close textured so I think it goes best with a fresh fruit compôte or some cream or dairy-free ice cream on the side.

50g soft dried mango (or soft dried pineapple or apricots)
juice and grated zest of 2 oranges
250g rice flour
50g coconut flour
50g polenta

2 tsp gluten-free baking powder
1 tsp bicarbonate of soda
1 tsp xanthan gum
3 large eggs
250g honey, plus extra to glaze
250g yogurt (I use fat-free)

50ml sunflower oil, plus extra for greasing
1 tsp vanilla extract
sunflower seeds, toasted, to decorate

1 Soak the mango in the orange juice and zest for an hour or so, or overnight.

2 Preheat the oven to 170°C/150°C fan/gas 3–4 and lightly grease a bundt tin or silicone bundt mould. If you're using a silicone mould, stand it on a baking sheet.

3 Put the rice flour, coconut flour and polenta in a large mixing bowl. Add the baking powder, bicarbonate of soda and xanthan gum and stir together.

4 In a separate mixing bowl, whisk the eggs with the honey, yogurt, sunflower oil and vanilla extract. Add the mango and its orange marinade and whisk this in.

5 Fold the egg mixture into the dry ingredients until there are no patches of flour, then spoon the batter into the bundt mould.

6 Bake for about 40–45 minutes until a skewer inserted in the deepest part of the cake comes out clean. The cake may bulge on top but you'll be able to level it when it cools. Leave it to cool in its tin or mould for a few minutes, and then pop it out to finish cooling on a wire rack.

7 To serve, trim the base to level it if you like, drizzle with a little more honey and decorate with the toasted sunflower seeds.

> **HOWARD'S TIP**
> Toast nuts or seeds in a dry pan over a medium heat, shaking the pan occasionally until they are browned, then tip them out of the pan straight away and leave to cool.

RHUBARB AND CUSTARD TARTS

Makes 12 tarts

Rhubarb and custard is a classic combination and it's nice to see the chunks of fruit sitting in these custard tarts. I like my rhubarb on the tart side (no pun intended), to contrast with the sweeter custard and pastry, but add sugar to the rhubarb for its initial baking if you prefer.

For the baked rhubarb
about 3 sticks of rhubarb
juice of $1/2$ orange
2 tsp caster sugar (optional)

For the pastry
150g rice flour, plus extra for rolling
50g quinoa flour
50g ground almonds
50g icing sugar
$1/4$ tsp gluten-free baking powder
a pinch of salt
1 tsp grated orange zest
125g cold unsalted butter, cubed (or dairy-free spread), plus extra for greasing
1 large egg
1 large egg white (use the yolk in the filling)

For the custard filling
4 large egg yolks
1 large egg
50g caster sugar
$1^1/2$ tbsp cornflour
300ml milk (dairy or non-dairy)
freshly grated nutmeg

1 Preheat the oven to 180°C/160°C fan/gas 4 and grease a 12-hole muffin tin.

2 Cut the rhubarb into 5cm (2in) chunks and put them in a baking dish. Drizzle with the orange juice and sprinkle with a little sugar, if you like. Bake for about 10 minutes until just tender, then leave to cool.

3 To make the pastry, mix together the flours, ground almonds, icing sugar, baking powder and a pinch of salt in large mixing bowl. Rub in the butter until there are no visible lumps.

4 Beat the egg and egg white together and add this to the mix, along with the orange zest, gathering the dough together with your hand until it forms a ball. Wrap in cling film and chill for 30 minutes.

5 On a floured work surface, roll out the pastry to about 4mm ($1/4$in) thick. Cut out circles about 10cm (4in) in diameter and use these to line the prepared muffin tin. (Keep any spare pastry in case you need to patch later). Pop the tart cases into the freezer for 15 minutes.

6 Place a paper muffin case inside each pastry shell, fill with baking beans and bake for 15 minutes. Carefully remove the beans and paper cases. If you spot any holes or cracks, you can do a repair job with tiny pellets of the spare pastry.

7 Turn the oven down to 160°C/140°C fan/gas 3.

8 Place a cooled rhubarb chunk inside each pastry case.

9 Make the custard by whisking together the eggs, sugar and cornflour in a large jug. Warm the milk slightly, and then pour this over the egg and sugar mix and whisk together. Fill the pastry cases with the custard and grate nutmeg generously on top.

10 Bake for about 12 minutes until the custard is set but still has a little wobble. Transfer to a wire rack to cool.

PLUM AND PECAN PIE WITH CONTINENTAL PASTRY

Makes a 26cm (10½in) pie

The Dutch apple pie that inspired my *Amsterdam apple cake* (see page 60) must have been a highly influential dessert. Its yeasted pastry gave me the idea of using a thin bread dough as the base for this pie, which is easily made dairy free. Ground pecans and maple syrup make a rich filling – serve chilled in thin slices.

For the pastry dough

250g gluten-free white bread flour blend, plus extra for rolling

50g sweet white sorghum flour

2 tsp quick yeast

1 tsp ground cinnamon

2 tbsp caster sugar

a pinch of salt

2 large eggs

100ml warm milk (dairy or non-dairy, like almond or oat)

6 tbsp mild and light olive oil

For the filling

3 large eggs

3 tbsp maple syrup

50g soft dark brown sugar

4 tbsp mild and light olive oil

200g ground pecans (or replace 100g with ground almonds)

For the topping

4 fresh plums (not too ripe)

about 40g pecan halves

1 Put the flours in a large mixing bowl and add the yeast, cinnamon, sugar and a pinch of salt.

2 Beat the 2 eggs with the warm milk and pour this into the dry ingredients. Add the 6 tbsp olive oil, stir to loosely combine, then cover the dough and leave it to rest at room temperature for 30 minutes or so.

3 Now make the filling – beat the eggs in a bowl with the maple syrup, brown sugar and 4 tbsp oil. Stir in the ground pecans with a wooden spoon.

4 Preheat the oven to 220°C/200°C fan/gas 7.

5 On a floured work surface, roll out the dough as thinly as you can, to line the base of a 26cm (10½in) round springform cake tin. You may need to do some firm coaxing of the dough to get it to go up the sides of the tin. With a sharp knife, trim the sides of the pastry case to about 3cm (1¼in) high.

6 Spoon the filling into the pastry case and spread it out evenly.

7 Cut the plums in half and remove the stones, then arrange them, skin-side up on top, pressing down gently. Place the pecan halves in the gaps.

8 Bake for 25 minutes until the filling is firm and risen. There may be a few signs of jammy juices just bubbling from some plums.

9 Leave to cool in the tin. Chill in the fridge before releasing from the springform to serve.

SPICED PEAR TART

Makes a 20cm (8in) tart

There's spice and rice in this pear tart, and the precious poaching liquor is reduced to a syrup for a glazed finish. Reading through the ingredients makes me think that, at some point, I may need to devise a healthier version of this tart. In the meantime, I trust you to cut very small slices.

For the spiced pears	For the pastry	For the filling
350ml white wine (or 50ml calvados and 300ml water)	150g rice flour, plus extra for rolling	50g unsalted butter
75g caster sugar	50g coconut flour	150ml double or whipping cream
3 star anise	50g oat flour	300ml milk
1 cinnamon stick	50g icing sugar	50g light brown muscovado sugar
2 firm pears, peeled, cored and quartered	a pinch of salt	$1/2$ tsp vanilla bean paste
juice of $1/2$ lemon	$1/4$ tsp gluten-free baking powder	$1/2$ tsp chai tea masala mix (I use The Spice Shop's)
1 tsp honey, to serve	125g cold unsalted butter, diced, plus extra for greasing	60g gluten-free ground rice
	1 tsp lemon zest	1 large egg
	1 large egg	1 large egg yolk
	1 large egg white (save the yolk for the filling)	

1 To poach the pears, heat the white wine (or calvados and water) and caster sugar in a large pan (such as a sauté pan) with the star anise and cinnamon stick. Bring to the boil, then simmer for 5 minutes. Add the prepared pears and lemon juice, cover the pan and cook for 10 minutes. Take off the heat and leave to cool.

2 To make the pastry, put the flours, icing sugar, salt and baking powder into a large mixing bowl. Rub the butter through until there are no visible lumps, then stir in the lemon zest. Whisk the egg and egg white and add to the flour mix. Stir through with a knife and then bring the dough together with your hands. Wrap the dough in cling film and chill until needed.

3 Preheat the oven to 180°C/160°C fan/gas 4 and pop a baking sheet in the oven to heat up. Lightly grease a 20cm (8in) springform cake tin.

4 On a lightly floured work surface, roll out the dough to 4mm (about $1/4$in) thick and use to line the prepared cake tin. You will need to patch the pastry if it cracks – you're aiming to cover the base and go part way up the sides.

5 With a sharp knife, trim the rim so the pastry case is about 4cm ($1^1/2$in) deep. At this point you can chill the pastry case in the fridge (or freezer) for a few minutes to firm it up again. (You will have some leftover pastry, so pop this back in the fridge and use to make jam tarts or whatever you fancy.)

6 Scrunch up a large piece of baking parchment, flatten it out, and use it to line the pastry case. Fill with baking beans and place the tin in the oven on top of the preheated baking sheet.

7 Bake for 20–25 minutes, then take it out of the oven, carefully remove the baking beans and parchment, then return it to the oven for a further 10 minutes until the surface of the pastry feels dryish. Take out of the oven and leave it to cool while you make the filling.

8 To make the filling, put the butter, cream, milk, brown sugar, vanilla and chai tea masala in a large pan. Bring to the boil, then turn it down to simmer and whisk in the ground rice. Keep whisking on the heat until the mixture thickens like a ground rice pudding.

9 Take the pan off the heat and whisk in the egg and egg yolk. Spoon the mixture into the pastry case, levelling it off with a wet knife or spatula. Arrange the pears on top, like the petals of a flower, gently pressing them in slightly. If the pears are long you may need to trim them just to get all the pieces in neatly.

10 Bake for 25 minutes until the filling is firm. Cool in the tin on a wire rack, and then chill in the fridge until needed.

11 To make the glazing syrup, remove the cinnamon stick and star anise from the poaching liquid and add the honey. Simmer vigorously for about 10 minutes, then take off the heat and leave it to cool and thicken.

12 To serve, remove the tart from its tin and brush the top with the spiced syrup.

HOWARD'S TIP
Make sure you check your packet of ground rice, as a major producer has warned that theirs is not gluten free because of cross contamination.

CRUNCHY NUT CARROT CAKES

Makes at least 12 cakes

Most carrot cakes and other vegetable-based cakes use oil not butter in the batter, so they're naturally dairy free. Then we go and ruin their credentials by plastering cream cheese frosting on top. This time I've used alternatives to the butter and cream cheese, so the little cakes stay dairy free. You can buy ready roasted and chopped hazelnuts but I think in this recipe it's nice to have some chunkier bits, plus you can use some of the whole roasted nuts for decoration.

For the cakes
75g dried pineapple, chopped into small chunks
grated zest and juice of 2 oranges
100g blanched hazelnuts (75g goes in the cake and the rest are for decoration)
125ml mild and light olive oil
125g muscovado sugar

3 large eggs, separated
75g nut butter, like almond, cashew or hazelnut
200g carrots, grated
75g gram flour
125g ground almonds
I tsp gluten-free baking powder
I tsp ground cinnamon

For the dairy-free frosting
225–255g tub of dairy-free tofu 'cream cheese'
125g dairy-free sunflower spread
125g icing sugar
grated zest of $^1/_2$ orange
$1^1/_2$ tsp orange juice

1 Put the pineapple pieces, orange zest and juice in a small bowl, cover and leave for an hour or so, or overnight.

2 Preheat the oven to 190°C/170°C fan/gas 5. Line a 12-hole muffin tin with paper cases.

3 Put the hazelnuts on a baking tray and roast them for a few minutes until lightly toasted. (Keep an eye on them and remember the bottom of the nuts will singe before the top.)

4 In a large mixing bowl, whisk the oil with the sugar, then add the egg yolks and nut butter. Roughly chop 75g of the roasted hazelnuts and add these to the mix, along with the grated carrots and the pineapple pieces and their orange marinade. Stir in the flour, ground almonds, baking powder and cinnamon and mix well.

5 In a separate bowl, whisk the egg whites until stiff, preferably using an electric hand-held mixer, then carefully fold them into the cake mixture so they are incorporated without losing too much air.

6 Divide the mixture among the muffin cases and bake for 20–25 minutes until firm and springy to the touch.

7 Let the cakes cool in the tin for a few minutes, then lift them out and cool on a wire rack.

8 To make the frosting, whisk half of the tofu 'cream cheese' with the sunflower spread and icing sugar until smooth. Add the rest of the 'cream cheese', along with the orange zest and juice and keep whisking until light and fluffy. Keep in the fridge until needed.

9 When the cakes are cold, spread or pipe the frosting on top and decorate with the remaining whole or chopped hazelnuts.

HOWARD'S TIP

Peanut butter used to be the only spreadable nut in town, but you can now see jars of almond, cashew, hazelnut, walnut and macadamia nut butter too. Seed butters are also appearing more – tahini (made from sesame seeds) has been around for centuries, but other seeds are now joining the crush – look out for sunflower and pumpkin seed butters for a start. Any of these will work in this recipe.

WALNUT AND DATE LOAF CAKE

Makes a 1.3kg (3lb) loaf

Everyone's heard of date and walnut cake, but this recipe really puts the walnuts first. It came about after I'd been a little over-enthusiastic with my nut grinding, in preparation for a class, and ended up with bags of leftover ground walnuts. It's a very moist, very walnutty cake – if you prefer something drier with a less intense walnut flavour, replace 100g of the ground walnuts with ground almonds or ground rice.

8 large eggs	200g pitted dates, chopped	1 tsp gluten-free baking powder
225g caster sugar	grated zest and juice of $\frac{1}{2}$ lemon	$\frac{1}{2}$ tsp ground cinnamon
1 apple, peeled, cored and coarsely grated (about 120g)	300g ground walnuts	
	75g chopped walnuts	

1 Preheat the oven to 190°C/170°C fan/gas 5 and line a 1.3kg (3lb) loaf tin with baking parchment.

2 In a large mixing bowl, whisk the eggs with the sugar, and then add all the other ingredients and stir with a wooden spoon until everything is combined.

3 Spoon the batter into the lined tin and bake for 45–55 minutes until firm and golden on top and a cake tester or skewer inserted in the middle comes out clean.

4 Cool in the tin for 15 minutes or so, then lift out the cake to finish cooling on a wire rack.

> **HOWARD'S TIP**
> Loaf tins are usually sized by weight and a 1.3kg (3lb) loaf tin measures 28x13x7cm ($11\frac{1}{4}$x5x$2\frac{1}{4}$in).

SWEDISH BUTTER BISCUITS

Makes 10–12 large biscuits

Traditionally made with potato flour – and usually with wheat flour too – these butter biscuits are also known as *uppåkra*, after a Swedish village. Take out the gluten, as I've done here, and you're left with an incredibly short-textured biscuit, delicate and delicious, but if you want them to reach your lips with more reliability, add a beaten egg white and a spot of guar gum to the mixture to give it strength.

220g unsalted butter, softened	220g potato flour	1 tsp vanilla bean paste
100g caster sugar	100g cornflour	grated zest of 1 lemon

1 Preheat the oven to 200°C/180°C fan/gas 6 and line a baking sheet with baking parchment.

2 In a large mixing bowl, cream the butter with the sugar until light and fluffy, then add the potato flour, cornflour, vanilla bean paste and lemon zest. Stir and knead until the dough comes together and all the flour has been absorbed.

3 Put large teaspoons of the mixture on a baking sheet and flatten them slightly. The biscuits sometimes spread, so leave a gap in between.

4 Bake for 15 minutes until golden brown at the edges. Let them cool on the tray a little before carefully transferring to a wire rack to finish cooling.

CHAPTER 3

FREE AND EASY

These recipes are quick to make and great for baking with kids. Though there are some shameless shortcuts in here, there are also some great basics to hopefully inspire the next generation of bakers.

NO-NUT BREAKFAST BARS

RASPBERRY AND WHITE CHOCOLATE SHORTBREAD

TROPICAL FLORENTINES

BANOFFEE BUFFINS

GINGER AND HONEY CORACLES

BLUEBERRY AND MANDARIN MADELEINES

COCONUT, PASSION FRUIT AND COCOA NIB BARS

SUMMER SWISS ROLL

POSH RICE CRISPY CAKES

LITTLE LEMON AND LIME CHEESECAKES

RASPBERRY AND RHUBARB ROULADE

EASY FREEZY CHOCOLATE TRUFFLES

COCONUT ICE WITH PENGUINS

SMOKED SALMON QUINOA QUICHES

CHEESE AND PICKLE MUFFINS

CHORIZO STRAWS

PIGS IN JACKETS

NO-NUT BREAKFAST BARS

Makes 12–16 bars

A crunchy way to start the day, and in this recipe there's no nut in nutritious.

40g coconut flour
40g flaxseed meal
40g chia seeds
40g gluten-free crispy puffed rice cereal

100g quinoa flakes
100g gluten-free oats
40g pitted dates
40g soft dried bananas

5 tbsp extra virgin olive oil
80g honey
60g coconut sugar

1 Preheat the oven to 180°C/160°C fan/gas 4 and line a 23x30cm (9x12in) baking tray or Swiss roll tin with baking parchment.

2 In a large mixing bowl, combine all the ingredients and stir with a wooden spoon until well mixed.

3 Tip the mixture into the prepared tin and press it down until it covers the base and is flat and even.

4 Bake for 20–25 minutes until firm on top. Using a sharp knife, score it into rectangular fingers or squares while it is still warm, and then leave it to cool and firm up in the baking tray.

5 Remove from the baking tray when cold and cut into bars. Store in an airtight tin, where it should keep for up to a week.

> **HOWARD'S TIP**
> If you're looking to reduce your intake of refined cane sugar, then coconut sugar has become a popular alternative. Made from the sap of the coconut palm, it has a caramel-like flavour and is lower in fructose than cane sugar. You can use it in place of brown sugar in most recipes – just remember, it is still a sugar so don't go overboard.

RASPBERRY AND WHITE CHOCOLATE SHORTBREAD

Makes about 16 shortbreads

It took several experiments to get this right, adjusting quantities, oven temperature, and so on. Every time, this so-called biscuit puffed up like a cake. About to give up, I discovered that the latest attempt had pulled itself together and firmed up on cooling, in time to avoid an imminent journey to the bin. Just in case this is actually a crucial part of its character-building process, I suggest you threaten your shortbread with a similar fate.

For the shortbread

150g unsalted butter

75g caster sugar

150g rice flour

75g gluten-free ground rice

1 tbsp icing sugar

10g freeze-dried raspberries

To decorate

about 50g organic white
   chocolate, broken into pieces

5g freeze-dried raspberries

1 Preheat the oven to 185°C/165°C fan/gas 4 and line a 22cm (8^1/2in) square tin with baking parchment.

2 In a large mixing bowl, cream the butter with the sugar and then add the rice flour, ground rice, icing sugar and freeze-dried raspberries and mix well. Spoon the mixture into the lined tin and press it down to compact it and make it level.

3 Bake for about 25 minutes until pale golden. During cooking, the shortbread will puff up like a cake and look disastrous. Even when it comes out of the oven it will still be too soft, but leave it to cool in the tin and it will eventually firm up enough for you to cut it into fingers.

4 When the shortbread is cold, melt the chocolate in a heatproof bowl in the microwave (or over a pan of simmering water).

5 Drizzle the melted chocolate over the shortbread fingers and sprinkle with more freeze-dried raspberries. Store in an airtight tin for up to 4 days.

TROPICAL FLORENTINES

Makes 8–10 Florentines

Tangy and coconutty – I think the hint of chilli in the chocolate makes all the difference.

50g unsalted butter (or dairy-free
   spread)
50g coconut sugar (or soft brown
   sugar)
3 tbsp pomegranate molasses

50g dried pineapple
25g dried mango
25g glacé cherries
50g Brazil nuts, chopped
25g coconut flour

grated zest of 1 lime
100g dark chocolate (use a dairy-
   free brand if needed), broken
   into pieces
$\frac{1}{2}$ tsp dried chilli flakes

1 Preheat the oven to 180°C/160°C fan/gas 4 and line a baking sheet with baking parchment.

2 Melt the butter with the sugar and pomegranate molasses in a pan over a low heat. Take the pan off the heat and add the pineapple, mango, cherries, nuts, coconut flour and lime zest and stir well to combine.

3 Drop spoonfuls of the mixture onto the lined baking sheet. This mixture doesn't spread like a traditional Florentine so you may need to flatten it now.

4 Bake for about 8 minutes until golden brown, then leave them to cool and firm up before removing from the parchment.

5 When the Florentines are cold, melt the chocolate in a heatproof bowl in the microwave (or over a pan of simmering water) and add the chilli flakes. Spread the melted chocolate on the back of the biscuits and let it set before serving. Store in an airtight tin for up to a week.

BANOFFEE BUFFINS

Makes 12 buffins

A cross between a bun and a muffin, these get their banoffee flavour from fresh and dried bananas, coupled with honey and muscovado sugar.

Banana recipes often call for overripe bananas, which is frustrating if you only have fairly fresh ones around. However, I've found you can 'distress' a banana – not by making it watch late-night horror movies, but by pummelling it to bruising point while it's still in its skin. Mashing the peeled fruit with honey also helps – creating a little more viscous liquid, if your bananas aren't up for producing it themselves.

Choose the soft, chewy dried bananas. If you can only get the crispy discs, soak them first in hot water … or in a suitable liqueur. Coffee liqueur is weirdly wonderful here.

3 medium bananas (about 300g in total), as ripe as possible or distressed if necessary	3 large eggs	1 tsp cinnamon
	100g light muscovado sugar	about 70g soft dried banana slices
	150g gluten-free oat flour	
4 tbsp honey	$^{1}/_{2}$ tsp bicarbonate of soda	
150ml mild and light olive oil	1 tsp xanthan gum	

1 Preheat the oven to 200°C/180°C fan/gas 6 and line a 12-hole muffin tin with paper cases.

2 In a large mixing bowl, mash the fresh bananas with the honey. Whisk in the oil, and then whisk in the eggs one at a time.

3 In a separate bowl, combine the sugar, oat flour, bicarbonate of soda, xanthan gum and cinnamon. Add this to the banana mixture and stir to form a batter.

4 Spoon a little of the batter into the prepared muffin cases, add one or two slices of dried banana in each, then top up with more batter. Finish off with another slice of dried banana.

5 Bake for 18–20 minutes until risen and springy to the touch.

6 Leave to cool in the tins a little, then remove and cool on a wire rack.

GINGER AND HONEY CORACLES

Makes up to 24 coracles

There's no shame in using kitchen equipment creatively. (Note to self – whatever you do – don't mention the incident with the balloon whisk at that party in Leeds.) Sometimes you look at a piece of bakeware, turn it over and an idea is born. Little pastry cases can be fiddly to get out of the tin intact, so what if you bake on the bottom of a mini muffin tin? These little shallow ginger biscuit boats are perfect for a fresh fruit filling.

230g rice flour, plus extra for rolling
120g potato flour
1 tsp bicarbonate of soda
1 tsp xanthan gum

2 tsp ground ginger
110g cold unsalted butter, cut into cubes (or dairy-free sunflower spread)
170g soft dark brown sugar

1 large egg
4 tbsp honey
fresh fruit and cream, or non-dairy alternative, to serve

1 Sift the flours, bicarbonate of soda, xanthan gum and ground ginger into a large mixing bowl and rub in the butter or sunflower spread until it is like breadcrumbs.

2 Stir in the brown sugar, then beat the egg with the honey and pour this in. Stir in the liquid with a knife, and then knead the mixture by hand in the bowl until it comes together as a soft dough.

3 Wrap the dough in cling film and chill for at least 30 minutes or until needed.

4 Preheat the oven to 190°C/170°C fan/gas 5 and line the underside of a mini muffin tin with paper cases. (I use a metal mini muffin tin with cupcake-sized paper cases, pressing them against the tin to fit.)

5 On a lightly floured work surface, roll out half the dough to about 6mm (^{1}/4in) thick, then stamp out circles, using a 7cm (2^1/4in) cutter. Rewrap the rest of the dough and reserve it for a second batch.

6 Place a disc of the dough on top of each paper case and bake for 10–12 minutes until golden brown.

7 Let the biscuits cool and firm up on the tin for a few minutes, then remove the paper cases as soon as they're cool enough to handle. Finish cooling on a wire rack.

8 When the cases are cold, fill them with fresh fruit and whatever creamy filling you like.

BLUEBERRY AND MANDARIN MADELEINES

Makes up to 12 madeleines

Many recipes for madeleines suggest you let the batter stand or chill before baking. Don't! In this gluten-free version, the xanthan and guar gums thicken the mix, so bake it immediately. You can also fill the moulds to the top without fear of overflow. Purists insist that madeleines should be eaten within an hour or so of baking. Maybe so, but, if stored in a tin, these taste fine to me the following day, if there are any still around.

100g unsalted butter, plus extra
   for greasing
2 large eggs
100g caster sugar
finely grated zest and juice of
   1 mandarin or $^1/_2$ orange

5 drops culinary bergamot oil
   (optional)
50g cornflour, plus extra for
   flouring the tin
50g rice flour
$^1/_2$ tsp baking powder

$^1/_2$ tsp xanthan gum
$^1/_4$ tsp guar gum
12 large blueberries

1 Preheat the oven to 210°C/190°C fan/gas 6–7. Lightly grease a madeleine tin (or silicone madeleine mould) and dust it with a little cornflour, then shake off any excess. If you are using a flexible silicone madeleine mould, place it on a baking sheet, so you'll be able to carry it to the oven more easily.

2 Melt the butter in a heatproof dish in the microwave or in a small saucepan on the hob, then leave it to cool a little.

3 In a large mixing bowl, whisk the eggs and sugar (preferably with an electric hand-held mixer) for a few minutes until they look like pale, smooth custard.

4 Add the melted butter, mandarin zest and juice, and bergamot oil (if using) and whisk these in, then whisk in the flours, baking powder and the gums to make a thick batter.

5 Spoon the batter into the moulds (or transfer it to a jug and pour it in), filling each indentation to about 2mm from the top. Place a fresh blueberry in the centre of each madeleine.

6 Bake for about 10 minutes until the cakes are light golden brown and the blueberries are just starting to release their juices.

7 Leave to cool a little in the tin, then release onto a wire rack. Eat while they're still warm, or leave to cool.

COCONUT, PASSION FRUIT AND COCOA NIB BARS

Makes 16 squares

Coconut, quinoa flakes and cocoa nibs combine to create a soft, crumbly biscuit and the passion fruit keeps it fresh and fruity.

75g rice flour

90g quinoa flakes (or gluten-free oats)

75g soft dark brown sugar

50g cocoa nibs

$^1/_4$ tsp gluten-free baking powder

50g desiccated coconut

a pinch of salt (optional)

75g unsalted butter (or dairy free spread), melted, plus extra for greasing

1 large egg

2 passion fruit (seeds and pulp)

1 Preheat the oven to 180°C/160°C fan/gas 4. Line a 23cm (9in) square baking tin with kitchen foil, so it comes over the sides of the tin, then lightly grease the foil.

2 In a large mixing bowl, put the rice flour, quinoa flakes, brown sugar, cocoa nibs, baking powder, coconut and a pinch of salt. Stir to combine.

3 In a separate bowl, whisk the melted butter with the egg and passion fruit, then add this to the dry ingredients and stir well.

4 Spoon the mixture into the lined tin and press it down so it's even.

5 Bake for 25 minutes until firm and golden. Remove from the tin by lifting the foil and cool on a wire rack. When it is cool, cut into 16 squares.

> **HOWARD'S TIP**
> Cocoa nibs are unprocessed cocoa beans, broken into pieces. You can buy them in health food stores or major supermarkets.

SUMMER SWISS ROLL

Makes a 23cm (9in) roll

This fatless sponge makes a beautifully light Swiss roll, ideal for filling with summer fruit and cream. Without the cream, it's naturally dairy free – if you want to keep it so, fill with jam or thick fruit compote. Alternatively, smear on dairy-free ice cream and fresh fruit for a more Arctic roll up.

For the sponge
2 large eggs, separated
85g caster sugar, plus extra for rolling
½ tsp vanilla extract or vanilla bean paste

25g rice flour
25g cornflour
½ tsp gluten-free baking powder

For the filling
250ml double cream
2 tsp freeze-dried raspberries or strawberries
100g fresh raspberries (or other soft fruit)

1 Preheat the oven to 180°C/160°C fan/gas 4 and line a 23x33cm (9x13in) Swiss roll tin with non-stick baking parchment.

2 In a large mixing bowl, whisk the egg yolks with the sugar until pale and creamy. (The mixture may turn sandy in texture at first, but keep whisking.)

3 In a separate bowl, whisk the egg whites until they are stiff.

4 Sift the flours and baking powder and stir this into the egg yolk mixture. Fold in the egg whites with a metal spoon, trying not to lose too much air.

5 Spoon the mixture on to the lined Swiss roll tin. It will seem like there isn't enough mixture – you need to spread it out evenly and patiently in what is a very thin layer.

6 Bake for 12–15 minutes until golden, risen and firm.

7 Whilst the sponge is in the oven, dampen two clean tea towels. Lay one of them out on the work surface, then put a sheet of baking parchment on top and dust it with caster sugar.

8 As soon as the sponge comes out of the oven, upturn it onto the sugared parchment. Now very carefully (and patiently again) remove the parchment it has been baked on. Don't worry too much about the odd bit that sticks, leaving a little crater – remember this is the unseen inside of the roll. Once you have removed the parchment it was baked on, cover the sponge with the second damp tea towel whilst you prepare the filling.

9 Whip the cream until stiff and wash the fesh fruit. Remove the top tea towel and spread cream on the sponge, then scatter on the freeze-dried fruit and then the fresh fruit. You may need to break up or squash the fresh berries a little if they are large.

10 Lifting the sugared baking parchment, start to roll up the sponge from one of the short edges, coaxing it over itself until it is rolled up fully.

11 Transfer to a serving plate or board and keep it cool in the fridge until you're ready to serve. You can dust it with a little more caster sugar before serving.

POSH RICE CRISPY CAKES

Makes about 20 of each type

'Petits fours' literally means little ovens – in this recipe, the little oven is a microwave. Like my *Chocolate bear buns* (see page 158), these evoke memories of kids' party food, but that's the very reason they're bound to raise a smile when you serve them to adults as an after-dinner treat. Use the very best quality ingredients and make the cakes in mini muffin cases.

For the white chocolate and
    cranberry cakes
100g organic white chocolate,
    chopped
50g unsalted butter
75g gluten-free crispy puffed rice
    cereal
50g dried cranberries

For the dark chocolate and ginger
    cakes
100g organic dark chocolate,
    chopped
50g unsalted butter
2 pieces of preserved stem ginger
    in syrup, drained and chopped
    (about 50g), or to taste
75g gluten-free crispy puffed rice
    cereal

1 To make the white chocolate and cranberry cakes, put the white chocolate and butter in a heatproof dish and heat in 30-second blasts in the microwave (it may only need a couple of blasts), then stir until the chocolate and butter are melted and the mixture is smooth.

2 Toss the puffed rice and cranberries in this mix, and then spoon it into the mini muffin cases and allow to set.

3 To make the dark chocolate and ginger cakes, put the dark chocolate and butter in a heatproof dish and heat in 30-second blasts in the microwave, then stir until the chocolate and butter are melted and the mixture is smooth.

4 Toss the ginger and puffed rice in the chocolate mix, and then spoon it into the mini muffin cases and allow to set.

LITTLE LEMON AND LIME CHEESECAKES

Makes 6 individual cheesecakes

These zingy little cheesecakes work beautifully with the biscuits used in the *Gingerbread theatre* recipe (see page 190), but you could use shop-bought gluten-free digestives. If you want to make them dairy free, remember that the ingredients in your biscuits must be dairy free too. I last made these with a lactose-free cream cheese, which was delicious, but you'll need to use a tofu-based substitute if you want them to be dairy free.

Making the jelly topping is a bit of a palaver, with so many limes to zest and juice, but it is worth it for that wonderfully tangy taste. If you're pushed for time, there are some good packet jelly crystals around that you could use instead.

For the lemon cheesecakes
150g gluten-free biscuits, such as digestives, or home-made gingerbread (see page 190)
50g dairy-free sunflower spread
200g dairy-free cream cheese substitute

1 tbsp caster sugar
1 tsp grated lemon zest
1 tsp lemon juice
1 large egg

For the lime topping
grated zest and juice of 5 limes
25g caster sugar
2–4 tsp agar flakes
extra lemon or lime zest, to decorate (optional)

1 Preheat the oven to 200°C/180°C fan/gas 6.

2 Crush the biscuits – you can do this by putting them in a plastic bag and crushing with a rolling pin, or by blitzing them in a food processor. Put the biscuit crumbs in a mixing bowl.

3 Melt the sunflower spread in a small pan or a heatproof bowl in the microwave, then add to the biscuit crumbs and stir together.

4 Press the mixture into the base of a 6-hole deep silicone muffin mould, then pop this into the freezer while you make the filling.

5 In a mixing bowl, beat the cream cheese substitute with the sugar, lemon zest, lemon juice and egg.

6 Take the muffin mould out of the freezer and place in on a baking sheet, then spoon the cream cheese mixture equally among the cases.

7 Bake for about 12–15 minutes until just set. Some may puff up and split a little but don't worry. Leave them to cool in the muffin mould.

8 When the cheesecakes are cold, make the jelly. Put the lime zest, lime juice and sugar in a small pan and heat gently until the sugar dissolves. Add 2 tsp agar flakes, turn up the heat and keep whisking for 3–4 minutes. Test if the jelly is setting by putting a little blob of it on a cold plate, leaving it for a minute or so, then pushing it with your finger. If it's not setting, add another 2 tsp agar flakes and whisk for a few more minutes.

9 Divide the jelly among the cheesecakes (you only need a thin layer on each one), then chill them in the fridge for an hour or so, or overnight.

10 To serve, run a thin blade knife around the edge of the cheesecakes, and then pop them out. Decorate with a little more lemon or lime zest, if you like.

RASPBERRY AND RHUBARB ROULADE

Makes a 23cm (9in) roulade

Impressive but actually fairly easy to make, this is a delicious dessert that you can adapt with whatever fruit is in season. It's best if you roll up as soon as you can after cooling. For a dairy-free option, try filling with the frosting from the *Crunchy nut carrot cakes* (see page 74).

For the baked rhubarb
3 sticks of rhubarb (about 300g), cut into 4cm (1¹/₂in) chunks
grated zest and juice of ¹/₂ orange
2 tsp caster sugar (optional)

For the roulade
4 large egg whites (or equivalent pasteurised egg white)
100g caster sugar
100g icing sugar, plus extra to finish
a pinch of salt
1 tsp of lime juice (about ¹/₂ lime)

1 tsp cream of tartar
50g chopped almonds

For the filling
75ml double cream
¹/₂ tsp vanilla extract
75ml fromage frais
about 100g fresh raspberries

1 To bake the rhubarb, preheat the oven to 200°C/180°C fan/gas 6.

2 Put the rhubarb in an ovenproof dish, squeeze over the orange juice and sprinkle on the zest and sugar (if using). Bake for 10–15 minutes until just soft but not mushy. Leave to cool.

3 Turn the oven down to 160°C/140°C fan/gas 3 and line a 23x33cm (9x13in) Swiss roll tin with baking parchment.

4 To make the roulade, in a large mixing bowl, whisk the egg whites to stiff peaks. Mix the caster sugar with the icing sugar and add this, a little at a time, whisking continuously until the mixture is thick, glossy and stiff. Add the salt, lime juice and cream of tartar and whisk them in.

5 Spoon the mixture into the lined tin and level it out. Sprinkle the chopped almonds on top.

6 Bake for 20 minutes until risen, the almonds are golden brown and the roulade is lightly coloured. Remove the roulade from the oven and turn it out onto a sheet of baking parchment. Carefully peel off the lining paper and let it cool for a few minutes.

7 To assemble, whip the cream with the vanilla extract until thick, then fold in the fromage frais. Spread this evenly on the back of the roulade, and scatter the raspberries and rhubarb on top.

8 Lifting the baking parchment under a short side of the roulade to help you, roll up the roulade, coaxing it over itself at first.

9 Lift it onto a serving plate and chill in the fridge until needed. Dust with a little icing sugar before serving.

EASY FREEZY CHOCOLATE TRUFFLES

Makes about 20 truffles

Dairy-free chocolate truffles that are a doddle to make and taste divine. Their only sin is that they don't like it hot ... or even room temperature to be honest. But serve them straight from the fridge, or better still the freezer, and you're blessed with perfectly heavenly after-dinner treats.

170g dairy-free chocolate (2 x 85g bars), chopped

4 tsp extra virgin olive oil

125ml non-dairy milk (such as coconut or hemp)

1 tsp coffee extract (or coffee liqueur) or other flavouring

a pinch of salt

about 25g organic cocoa powder

coffee beans and gold leaf to decorate (optional)

1 Put the chocolate in a large heatproof bowl with the olive oil, non-dairy milk, coffee extract (or other chosen flavouring) and a pinch of salt. Microwave on 750W for 30 seconds, then stir until there are virtually no lumps of chocolate left. Microwave for another 15 seconds, then stir until smooth.

2 Cover the bowl and chill it in the fridge overnight.

3 To make truffle balls, scoop out the mixture using a melon baller. If the mixture is still too soft to handle, pop it in the freezer to firm up.

4 Roll the truffles in cocoa powder and keep them in the fridge or freezer until it's time to serve. If you're feeling very fancy, you can decorate them with gilded coffee beans.

COCONUT ICE WITH PENGUINS

Makes about 49 cubes of coconut ice and 3 penguins

Coconut ice is so easy that I felt obliged to justify its inclusion with added penguins. Together they make a pretty cool Antarctic landscape that would also look great atop a special-occasion cake. If you are impatient and want to assemble this as soon as it is ready, then simply make the penguins first.

For the coconut ice
397g can of condensed milk
250g icing sugar
270 desiccated coconut
5g freeze-dried raspberries, crushed
5–10g freeze-dried blackberries, crushed

For the penguins
250g white sugar modelling paste
yellow edible dusting powder
black edible paint

1 Line an 18cm (7in) square baking tin with baking parchment.

2 In a bowl, mix the condensed milk with the icing sugar and stir in the coconut.

3 Divide the mixture in half, then add the crushed raspberries to one half and the crushed blackberries to the other half.

4 Spread the blackberry layer in the tin and level it out, then top with the raspberry layer and level this too. Cover the tin with cling film and leave it to set overnight at room temperature before you cut it into blocks the size of ice cubes. Store in an airtight tin until ready to serve.

5 To make each penguin, take about a quarter of the modelling paste, roll it into a ball to soften it, then mould it into a cone shape by rolling it between your hands. Roll the top of the cone as thin as you can, then bend it over to form the penguin's beak.

6 Flatten a piece of the modelling paste (either by rolling it with a small rolling pin or just pressing it down firmly) and cut out a thin crescent shape to make its wings. Press this firmly on the penguin's back.

7 Cut out two tiny triangles for its feet. If you're fussy about detail, you can get a good webbed effect with a small fluted pastry cutter. On a small board lined with baking parchment, place the feet about 1cm ($^{1}/_{2}$in) apart and sit the penguin on top of them.

8 Make another two penguins with the rest of the modelling paste, then leave them to dry fully, at least overnight but a couple of days is better.

9 With a clean small paintbrush, apply yellow dusting powder to the beak. It's best to do this with the beak pointing down so you don't get yellow on the penguin's tummy. Stand the penguin upright again and apply dusting powder to its feet.

10 With another clean small paintbrush, paint the penguin's wings and back with the black edible paint. Dot in its eyes and leave to dry.

11 Arrange the blocks of ice on a serving board and let the penguins begin colonising their coconut home.

SMOKED SALMON QUINOA QUICHES

Makes 6 large muffin-sized quiches

These pastry-free quiches use a spoonful of pre-cooked quinoa to create a hint of a crust, but their heritage is just as much omelette or soufflé as it is quiche. Classic smoked salmon accompaniments of dill and pickles add a Nordic flavour but fresh parsley and sundried tomatoes make a nice alternative.

a little olive oil for greasing

50g pre-cooked quinoa

6 large eggs

100ml milk

2 tsp capers, drained

4–5 pickled cornichons, drained and sliced

a small handful of fresh dill (about 10g), chopped

freshly ground black pepper

100g smoked salmon, cut or torn into small pieces

50g Cheddar cheese, grated

1 Preheat the oven to 190°C/170°C fan/gas 5 and lightly oil a 6-hole silicone muffin tray. Stand the muffin tray on a baking sheet to make it easier to move it to the oven when it's time to bake.

2 Spoon the pre-cooked quinoa into the muffin holes, sharing it equally.

3 Whisk the eggs and milk together in a jug, then add the capers, sliced cornichons, chopped dill, and season with black pepper. Stir in the pieces of salmon and grated cheese. Pour the mixture into the muffin tray.

4 Bake for 30 minutes until the quiches are puffed up (they sink back on cooling), firm and golden.

HOWARD'S TIP

You can now buy dried pre-cooked quinoa, which only needs reviving with hot water. In this recipe, I use it straight from the packet, so the savoury custard moistens it to form a crust. If you can only find uncooked quinoa, you'll need to rinse it in a sieve, then cook it in a pan (1 part quinoa to 3 parts water) for about 20 minutes until the quinoa has absorbed all the water.

CHEESE AND PICKLE MUFFINS

Makes 12 muffins

Show these simple muffins a good time – I like to use a good cheese, a great pickle and top them with Borettane onions in balsamic vinegar (look out for them – they are Italian onions with a flatter shape), just to make them feel extra special. But that's the kind of guy I am.

75g gram flour	1 tsp xanthan gum	2 tbsp pickle (a fine texture is best
75g cornflour	1 tsp mustard powder (optional)	– I like Stokes Sticky Pickle)
50g potato flour	125ml fat free yogurt	125g mature cheese, such as strong
50g polenta	125ml milk (skimmed is fine)	Cheddar or Red Leicester
2 tsp gluten-free baking powder	2 large eggs	6 pickled onions, halved (optional)
1/2 tsp bicarbonate of soda	100ml mild and light olive oil	

1 Preheat the oven to 210°C/190°C fan/gas 6–7 and line a 12-hole muffin tin with paper muffin cases.

2 Mix the dry ingredients together in a large mixing bowl.

3 Put the yogurt in a measuring jug, then top up with milk to the 250ml mark. Add the eggs, oil, pickle and 100g of the cheese and mix well.

4 Pour this into the dry ingredients and gently combine using a wooden spoon. Don't over-mix, but just check there are no patches of flour lurking at the bottom of the bowl.

5 Spoon into the muffin cases, top with half a pickled onion and a little more grated cheese and bake for 20 minutes until golden brown.

6 Transfer to a wire rack. Leave the muffins to cool completely if you want to be able to peel off the paper cases easily.

CHORIZO STRAWS

Makes 30 straws

This attempt to laminate with chorizo – creating savoury layers of pastry – may get a little untidy, but it's still very tasty. (It also makes a great top crust for a chicken pie.) What you end up with is something not unlike a spicy, meaty, garibaldi biscuit. Having gone to the trouble of carefully rolling and folding to entrap the sausage slices, it occurred to me later that you'd probably get much the same flavour if you just chop your chorizo and mix it in with the pastry. The chorizo choice is yours.

150g wholegrain brown rice flour, plus extra for rolling	¼ tsp gluten-free baking powder	1 large egg
50g gram flour	100g cold unsalted butter, cubed	1 large egg white (save the yolk for glazing)
50g cornflour	25g fresh Parmesan cheese, grated	100g cooked chorizo slices
50g gluten-free pinhead oats	1 tsp dried oregano	
	1 tsp smoked paprika	

1 In a large mixing bowl, mix the flours, oats and baking powder, then rub in the butter until there are no visible lumps. Stir in the grated Parmesan cheese, the oregano and paprika.

2 Whisk the egg and egg white and add to the flour mix. Stir it in with a knife, then bring the dough together with your hands.

3 On a lightly floured work surface, roll out the dough to about 30x25cm (12x10in). Cover with slices of chorizo, then fold the ends in – it may crack, but don't panic too much. Roll out again, and repeat. Wrap the dough in cling film and chill it for 10 minutes.

4 Preheat the oven to 210°C/190°C fan/gas 6–7 and line a baking sheet with baking parchment.

5 Roll out the dough to about 30cm (12in) square – aim to go as thin as you dare. Now, with a very sharp knife or pizza wheel, slice it into fingers 15cm (6in) long – you should get 30 in total.

6 Carefully transfer the slices to the lined baking sheet. Brush with the leftover egg yolk and bake for 15–20 minutes until firm and golden. Cool on a wire rack.

PIGS IN JACKETS

Makes 6–8 little pigs

Most parties have their pigs in blankets, cowering under puff pastry – inappropriate attire in my book – I thought it was high time they smartened up and put on a jacket. Crispy fried sage leaves make perfect pigs' ears, though Peter did think they were rabbits. There's an alternative recipe in there somewhere.

2 tbsp extra virgin olive oil

12–16 sage leaves

3–4 small potatoes (about
    120–140g each)

400g gluten-free sausage meat
    (most likely the filling of 6
    gluten-free sausages)

1 tsp tomato purée (optional)

6–8 slices of pitted black olives

1 Heat the oil in a smallish saucepan over a medium heat. When it's hot, drop a few sage leaves into the pan. Use a wooden skewer or something similar to encourage them to stay flat in the oil. When a leaf stops bubbling on one side, turn it over with a fork. Remove the leaves and place on kitchen paper, where they will dry out and crisp up. Store in an airtight container until needed.

2 Preheat the oven to 210°C/190°C fan/gas 6–7.

3 Wash and prick the potatoes, then bake them for about 1 hour (depending on size) until the middle feels fairly soft – it will give when pressed.

4 Leave to cool a little, then slice them in half and scoop out the potato middle to leave the skins. You can mix some of this potato flesh with the sausage meat, (along with a little tomato purée) which means that the meat will stretch further, or use it in another recipe like the *Two-potato farls* (see page 32) or *Hot potatoes* (see page 124).

5 In a small bowl, mash the sausage meat with a fork to loosen it up. Fill the potato skins with the sausage meat and put them in a baking dish or tin. Bake for about 25 minutes (you can check the exact recommended time for cooking a sausage on the packet, and adjust the oven temperature if necessary) until the meat is cooked through.

6 When cooked, make two small incisions with a sharp knife and insert two of the crispy sage leaves to make the pig's ears. Add a slice of black olive for its snout. Serve warm or cold.

CHAPTER 4

FANCY FREE

Sometimes, the time is right to do a bit of showing
off – special occasions demand tasty nibbles,
and everyone likes a showstopper or two.

FIG AND FETA TARTLETS

Makes 12 tartlets

Sweet, juicy figs contrast perfectly with the salty tang of feta. Serve the little tartlets as substantial finger food, a dinner party starter with a light salad, or even at the end of a meal in place of cheese and biscuits.

For the pastry	$^1/_4$ tsp gluten-free baking powder	For the filling
150g wholegrain rice flour, plus extra for rolling	100g cold unsalted butter, cubed	70g pre-cooked quinoa
50g quinoa flour	30g fresh Parmesan cheese, grated	200ml boiling water
50g potato flour	freshly ground black pepper	100g feta cheese, crumbled
50g gluten-free pinhead oats	1 large egg	1 tsp fresh thyme leaves
	1 large egg white (save the yolk for the filling)	1 large egg yolk
		3 fresh figs, quartered

1 In a large mixing bowl, put the flours, pinhead oats and baking powder and stir to combine. Rub in the butter until there are no visible lumps, then stir in the grated Parmesan and black pepper.

2 Whisk the egg and egg white and stir them in with a knife, then bring the dough together with your hands.

3 On a floured work surface, roll out the dough to 4mm (about $^1/_4$in) thick (it's easiest to do this in two batches), then stamp out circles using a 10cm (4in) cutter and line a 12-hole muffin tin. Patch any cracks with pellets of pastry, then put the tin in the freezer for 20 minutes.

4 Preheat the oven to 210°C/190°C fan/gas 6–7, and pop in a baking sheet to heat up.

5 Put a paper muffin case inside each pastry shell and fill with baking beans. Bake for about 12 minutes, then remove the beans and paper cases and bake for a further 5 minutes to dry off the pastry. Let the pastry cases cool in the tin while you prepare the filling.

6 Put the pre-cooked quinoa in a bowl and pour oven 200ml of boiling water. Let it stand for 3–5 minutes so the quinoa absorbs most of the water. Drain in a sieve, if necessary.

7 Mix the quinoa with the feta cheese, thyme leaves and egg yolk. Spoon the mixture into the pastry cases, and then put a piece of fig in each tartlet, pressing it gently into the filling.

8 Bake for about 10 minutes until the figs are just starting to release their juices. Serve the tartlets warm or cold.

> **HOWARD'S TIP**
> In my Smoked salmon quinoa quiches (see page 108), I use pre-cooked and dried quinoa straight from the packet. In this recipe it's revived with hot water.

RED ONION BHAJIS

Makes about 30 bhajis

The first of my three Indian-inspired canapés, these bhajis include chillies and sundried tomatoes for extra redness with the onions. Rice flour and egg whites add a hint of tempura crispness to the traditional gram-flour batter.

150g gram flour

50g rice flour

2 large egg whites (or equivalent pasteurised egg white)

about 200ml cold water

3 red onions, peeled and finely sliced, and any long pieces cut again

about 8 sundried tomatoes in oil, drained, patted dry with kitchen roll, then chopped

2 red chillies, finely chopped

2 tsp roasted curry blend powder

2 tsp cumin seeds

a pinch of salt (optional)

sunflower oil for deep frying

1 Sift the flours into a large mixing bowl.

2 Whisk the egg whites until frothy, then add them to the flour and gradually whisk in enough of the water to make a smooth, creamy batter.

3 Now add the sliced red onions, chopped sundried tomatoes, red chillies and spices, along with a pinch of salt, if you like.

4 Preheat the oven to 120°C/100°C fan/gas ½ – just so you can keep the cooked bhajis warm.

5 Pour the sunflower oil into a deep pan or wok so it's about 5cm (2in) deep. Heat the oil then test it with a blob of batter – it will sizzle and float and start to brown when the oil is hot enough.

6 Drop spoonfuls of the batter into the hot oil and fry a few bhajis for about 4 minutes until crisp and golden, turning them over with a strainer to make sure they're cooked all round.

7 Drain on kitchen paper and keep warm in the oven while you cook the remaining bhajis.

INDIAN CANAPÉS
CAULIFLOWER CHEESE FRITTERS

Makes 20 fritters

If you want to make them sound more authentic, I suppose you could call these fritters *gobi paneer*. My time spent reading Indian restaurant menus has not been wasted.

200g cauliflower florets

1 tsp cumin seeds (or ¹/₂ tsp cumin powder)

225g pack of paneer cheese, coarsely grated

grated zest of ¹/₂ lemon

2 garlic cloves, peeled and thinly sliced

1 tsp grated fresh root ginger

2 large eggs

2 tbsp gram flour

sunflower or rice bran oil, for frying

1 Preheat the oven to 240°C/220°C fan/gas 9 and line a baking tray or roasting tin with kitchen foil.

2 Put the cauliflower florets in a roasting tin, sprinkle with the cumin and roast for about 15 minutes until charred.

3 Break up any large florets, tip the cauliflower and cumin into a large bowl and mix with the paneer cheese, lemon zest, garlic, ginger, eggs and gram flour.

4 Take large teaspoons of the mix and shape into little patties by hand. Chill until ready to cook.

5 Heat the oil in a non-stick frying pan over a medium heat. Fry the fritters a few at a time for 2–3 minutes until they are golden brown on one side, and then turn over to cook the other side. Drain on kitchen paper. Keep them warm in a low oven while you fry the remaining fritters.

INDIAN CANAPÉS
HOT POTATOES

Makes about 40 snacks

Dairy free, egg free, nut free, low in fat and the salt is optional – how virtuous can a snack be? Well, be warned – it's the quiet ones you need to watch out for. They may seem small and innocently spiced at first but wait until the tongue-tingling mustard seeds and chilli flakes kick in! Best make lots – once your tongue has recovered, they're bound to be a talking point.

1 tbsp sunflower oil	$^1/_2$ tsp dried red chilli flakes	grated zest of $^1/_2$ lemon
2 tsp black mustard seeds	$^1/_2$ tsp roasted curry powder blend	2 heaped tbsp gram flour, plus extra for rolling
1 small red onion, finely chopped	500g mashed potato (from about 4 small-medium sized potatoes)	a pinch of salt (optional)
2 garlic cloves, peeled and finely chopped		

1 Preheat the oven to 220°C/200°C fan/gas 7 and line two baking sheets with baking parchment.

2 Heat the oil in a pan over a low-medium heat and gently fry the mustard seeds, onion, garlic, chilli flakes and curry powder for 5 minutes, or until the onion and garlic are softened.

3 Add this, including any residual oil, to the mashed potato. Stir in the lemon zest, gram flour and add a pinch of salt, if you like. Mix well with a wooden spoon and clump it together with your hand.

4 Tip the dough out on to a lightly floured work surface and roll it out to about 4mm (about $^1/_4$in) thick. Stamp out discs using a 4–5cm (1$^1/_2$–2in) round cutter and transfer them to the lined baking sheet. Re-roll until you have used all the dough.

5 Bake for 15 minutes until golden brown and crisp. These are best served quickly, as they soon soften (even in an airtight tin), though they are still amazingly tasty!

CHINESE CANAPÉS
SESAME PRAWN CRACKLERS

Makes about 20 cracklers

An up-market version of sesame prawn toasts, these tasty canapés also drew inspiration from sesame brittle. Icing sugar might seem odd in a savoury recipe but with the lime it's really just a touch of sweet and sour. The biscuits crackle enticingly as they cool – hence the name.

For the cracklers	For the topping
vegetable oil, for greasing	20 raw king prawns, shelled
1 large egg white	1 tbsp gluten-free sweet chilli
25g icing sugar	sauce, plus extra for serving
25g rice flour	1 tsp sesame oil
130g sesame seeds	1 tsp grated lime zest (optional)
a pinch of Fleur de Sel salt	1 or 2 fresh chillies, very finely
$^1/_2$ tsp ground ginger	sliced into rings (optional)

1 Preheat the oven to 170°C/150°C fan/gas 3–4. Line a baking sheet with baking parchment and grease the parchment with vegetable oil.

2 In a bowl, mix the egg white, icing sugar, rice flour, sesame seeds, salt and ground ginger.

3 Spoon blobs of the mixture onto the baking sheet, flattening the mixture with the spoon or a wet finger. You can leave the shapes ragged or use a small round cutter (about 4cm (1$^1/_2$in)) to tidy them up, gathering any excess mixture outside the circle and re-using.

4 Bake for 12 minutes until golden, and then remove from the oven. Listen to them crackle as they firm up if you have nothing better to do.

5 Leave to cool and stabilise before removing them from the baking sheet. They come off the paper best when cool, but not completely cold.

6 To make the topping, toss the prawns in the sweet chilli sauce and sesame oil. Fry the prawns in a large non-stick pan, turning them once, until just cooked on both sides. Remove them from the pan as soon as they are cooked so they don't shrink too much.

7 Place a prawn on each biscuit and decorate with strands of lime zest and rings of chilli, if you like. Serve with more sweet chilli sauce on the side.

CHINESE CANAPÉS
FIVE-SPICE SALMON CAKES

Makes about 40 cakes

A spiced, rösti-style fishcake that's best served crisp and hot. I leave the salmon skin on because I like its crispy strands among the potatoes. I may be alone here – skin the fish before slicing, if you prefer.

I fresh boneless salmon piece (about 150g), with or without skin

I tsp Chinese rice vinegar

1/2 tsp Chinese five-spice powder

550g potatoes (I used Duke of York)

3 large egg whites (or equivalent pasteurised egg white)

2 tbsp rice flour

1/2 tsp bicarbonate of soda

3 large spring onions, finely sliced

I tsp fresh root ginger, finely sliced or chopped

rice bran oil or sunflower oil, for frying

1 Place the salmon in a shallow dish. Mix the rice vinegar with the five-spice powder and rub this into the fish. Cover and chill in the fridge while you prepare the potatoes.

2 Peel and grate the potatoes into a sieve over a pan or bowl. With a large spoon, press down on the grated potatoes to squeeze out any excess liquid.

3 Slice the salmon as thinly as you possibly can. It's probably best to do this by cutting it in half lengthways, and then in slivers across.

4 In a large bowl, whisk the egg whites with the rice flour and bicarbonate of soda, then add the spring onions and fresh ginger. Add the sliced salmon and grated potatoes and mix well to combine.

5 Heat a little oil in a wok or non-stick frying pan over a medium heat.

6 Drop teaspoons of the mixture into the pan. Flatten them with the back of a spoon – aim for thin, lacy Florentines, even at the expense of uniformity. Cook for about 5 minutes on each side until golden and crisp and the potato is cooked through.

7 Drain on brown paper (this absorbs residual fat and keeps them crisp) and keep them warm until you are ready to serve.

CHINESE CANAPÉS
STICKY RICE CRAB CAKES

Makes 6 crab cakes about 7cm (2³/4in) in diameter

Glutinous rice flour is usually used to make a sweet Chinese dessert: sticky little fried cakes filled with nuts and drizzled with honey. Here, I've gone for a savoury twist, with fresh crabmeat and pickled ginger. The very soft, sticky quality of glutinous rice flour (which is still gluten free, by the way) is not everyone's cup of Oolong, but I think it's worth giving it a go.

For the dough
200g glutinous rice flour
about 200ml cold water

For the filling
100g crab meat (I use Seafood and Eat It's Cornish White Crab or their 50–50 Crab)
1 tsp chopped root ginger in white wine vinegar, well drained
1 tsp finely sliced spring onion

rice bran oil or sunflower oil, for frying

1 To make the dough, put the glutinous rice flour in a large mixing bowl, add about half of the water and mix it with your hand – clumping and kneading the dough to bring it together. Add more water, a little at a time, and keep working it until you have a smooth, cohesive ball of dough that feels like clay or firm fondant icing. Wrap it in cling film to stop it drying out while you make the filling.

2 Mix the crab meat with the drained chopped ginger and spring onion. It's important to have as little moisture as possible in the filling, so it's best to let the mixture sit in a sieve over a bowl.

3 Dampen your hands, divide the dough into 6 pieces and wrap 5 in cling film. Take the other piece (wetting your hands occasionally under the cold tap), roll the dough into a ball, then press your thumb into the centre and make a little pocket for the crab filling.

4 Put a little of the filling (no more than 1 tsp) inside, then bring the dough over to hide the filling inside. Now flatten the dough ball ready for cooking. (The drier your filling, the less chance there is of anything squelching out at this stage). Repeat with the rest of the dough and filling. Keep the expectant cakes under a clean damp cloth, ready for frying.

5 When you're ready to cook, heat a little oil in a wok or large non-stick frying pan over a medium-high heat. Fry the cakes for about 3 minutes on each side until gold and lightly charred. Serve warm.

PORTUGUESE SARDINE TART

Makes a 20x30cm (8x12in) shallow tart

Is it just me who looks at a rectangular baking tin with rounded corners and sees a tin of sardines? Well that's how this recipe started. It's not authentically Portuguese, of course, but by using indigenous sardines in the filling and piri piri in the crust, I might just get away with it.

For the pastry
150g tapioca flour, plus extra for rolling
50g millet flour
50g potato flour
50g gluten-free pinhead oats
1/4 tsp gluten-free baking powder

1/4 tsp guar gum
100g cold unsalted butter, cubed
30g fresh Parmesan cheese, grated
2 tsp piri piri seasoning (I like The Spice Shop's as it has no salt)
1 large egg
1 large egg white (use the yolk for glazing)

For the filling
2 x 135g tins of Portuguese sardines in tomato sauce (such as Conserverie Parmentier)
400g tin of chopped tomatoes, drained
1 tbsp polenta
8–10 cherry tomatoes, halved horizontally
1 pitted black olive, sliced
1 large egg yolk, for glazing

1 To make the pastry, put the flours and pinhead oats in a large mixing bowl and stir in the baking powder and guar gum. Rub in the butter until there are no visible lumps, then stir in the grated Parmesan and piri piri seasoning.

2 Whisk the egg and egg white until frothy, and then add this to the dry ingredients. Stir through with a knife, and then bring the dough together with your hand. Wrap in cling film and chill until needed.

3 Place two long strips of folded baking parchment in the bottom of a 20x30cm (8x12in) anodised aluminium baking tray (or similar). The strips need to form a cross and be longer than the length and width of the tin – these will help with removing the tart from its tin after baking.

4 On a floured surface, roll out the pastry to a thickness of 4mm (about 1/4in) and line the tin, covering the base and coming up the sides. This is easier said than done – even with the addition of a little guar gum, this is still a fragile pastry, so you'll inevitably need to patch it to get an even coverage.

5 Using a sharp knife, trim the sides of the pastry case so they are about 2–3cm (1in) high all round. Save the trimmed and leftover pastry for decoration. Pop the pastry case in the fridge for 30 minutes, or the freezer for 10 minutes.

6 Preheat the oven to 180°C/160°C fan/gas 4.

7 Make the filling by mashing the sardines and tomato sauce with the drained tinned tomatoes. Sprinkle a little polenta in the bottom of the chilled pastry case, then spoon the filling on top and level it out so it covers the base.

8 Roll out the leftover pastry and cut three long sardine shapes. Lay them carefully on top of the filling. Press the halved cherry tomatoes, cut-side up, in between the pastry sardines. Brush the pastry sardines with a little of the leftover egg yolk, then place a slice of olive on each of them, to make the sardines' eyes.

9 Bake for 35–40 minutes until the pastry case has shrunk slightly from the sides and the pastry sardines on top have a nice golden glow. Leave to cool in the tin, then chill in the fridge until you're ready to serve.

HOWARD'S TIP

There's a knack to turning this out and it's easier with two people. I wiggle and slide the paper strips to ensure the pastry case is released underneath, but I'm not confident enough to use them to actually lift the tart out of its tin. First get your serving platter or board nearby. Now find a small tray, chopping board or hard book (you can cover this in cling film if you're concerned about hygiene) that fits into the tin with a little gap, and then hold this against the top of the tart. Carefully, but confidently, upturn the tart (get your assistant to lift off the tin), then place the serving platter against the base of the tart and turn it right way up again.

SEVILLE ORANGE TART

Makes a 23cm (9in) fluted tart

The Spanish *tarta di Santiago* consists of ground almonds, eggs and sugar, not unlike a Bakewell tart, but while the demure Bakewell keeps its fruits under cover, my shady dame from Seville has hers on display. Seasonal Seville slices are candied and arranged like the vaulted ceilings of the Alcazar palace. Well, maybe that's a bit excessive – this is essentially a tart topping of chunky marmalade.

For the candied oranges
3 Seville oranges
about 1 litre cold water
250g caster sugar

For the pastry
150g rice flour, plus extra for rolling
50g gram flour
125g cold unsalted butter, cubed (or dairy-free spread)

50g ground almonds
50g icing sugar
1 tsp ground cinnamon
$1/4$ tsp gluten-free baking powder
a pinch of salt
1 large egg
1 large egg white (save the yolk for the filling)

For the filling
125g unsalted butter, softened (or dairy-free spread)
125g caster sugar
2 large eggs
1 large egg yolk
125g rice flour
$1/2$ tsp gluten-free baking powder
$1/2$ tsp xanthan gum
125g ground almonds

To finish
a few pine nuts (optional)

1 Wash the oranges and slice them about 5mm ($1/4$in) thick. Place them in a large shallow frying pan or sauté pan with the water, bring to the boil and simmer with the lid on for about 30-40 minutes until the peel of the oranges is softened and the white pith has become translucent. Carefully remove the orange slices, pick out and discard the pips.

2 Strain the water to remove any floating pips and measure out about 400ml of the water. Put this back in the pan with the sugar and orange slices.

3 Bring to the boil and simmer fairly vigorously (without the lid now) until the sugar has dissolved and the water has thickened into a syrup. You can let this syrup caramelise but take care not to let the orange slices disintegrate too much. Take the pan off the heat and leave it to cool while you make the pastry.

4 Put the flours in a large mixing bowl, then rub in the butter until there are no visible lumps. Stir through the ground almonds, icing sugar, cinnamon, baking powder and a pinch of salt.

5 Beat the egg and egg white and stir this into the bowl, then gather the dough by hand until it forms a ball. Wrap it in cling film and chill for 30 minutes.

6 Preheat the oven to 180°C/160°C fan/gas 4 and pop in a baking sheet to heat up.

7 On a floured work surface, roll out the pastry to 5mm (¹/₄in) thick and use it to line a 23cm (9in) fluted, loose-bottom tart tin. (You will have some leftover pastry so pop this back in the fridge and use it to make jam tarts or whatever else you fancy.)

8 Scrunch up a piece of baking parchment, then flatten it out and use it to line the pastry case. Fill with baking beans and put the pastry case on top of the hot baking sheet. Bake it for about 20 minutes, then carefully remove the baking beans and parchment and bake for a further 10 minutes until the surface of the pastry feels dryish. Take out of the oven and leave to cool a little while you make the topping.

9 In a mixing bowl, cream together the butter and sugar. Beat the eggs and egg yolk and add these a little at a time, alternating with a little rice flour.

10 Stir in the baking powder, xanthan gum, ground almonds and the rest of the rice flour. Mix well, and then spoon this into the pastry case. Arrange the candied orange slices on top. Use pine nuts to replace the pips, if you like.

11 Bake for about 30 minutes until firm and risen and a skewer inserted into the centre comes out clean. Cool on a wire rack before removing the tart from its tin.

MOCHACCINO WAFER CAKE

Makes a 20cm (8in) cake

A real barista-style creamy coffee cake – this even comes with its own wafers.

For the wafers

2 egg whites

65g caster sugar

50g roasted chopped hazelnuts, ground

25g cornflour

25g unsalted butter, melted

For the cake

30g organic cocoa powder

20g instant espresso powder

2 tsp coffee extract (or coffee liqueur)

about 150ml boiling water

180g light brown muscovado sugar

150ml mild and light olive oil

3 eggs

100g roasted chopped hazelnuts, ground

50g roasted chopped hazelnuts

3 tbsp chestnut flour (or other gluten-free flour)

$1/2$ tsp bicarbonate of soda

To finish

200ml double cream

1 tsp vanilla extract or vanilla bean paste

a little maple syrup, to decorate (optional)

1 Preheat the oven to 180°C/160°C fan/gas 4. Cut out 2 x 20cm (8in) circles of baking parchment (or use pre-cut non-stick cake liners) and put them on a baking sheet.

2 To make the wafers, whisk the egg whites in a large mixing bowl for a few seconds, then add the sugar and whisk until fairly thick and creamy. Fold in the hazelnuts, cornflour and melted butter.

3 Spread the mixture over the parchment circles and bake for 20 minutes. Leave the wafers to cool on a wire rack.

4 To make the cake, line 2 x 20cm (8in) springform cake tins with baking parchment.

5 Mix the cocoa with the espresso powder, and add the coffee extract and enough boiling water to make a thin paste.

6 Put the sugar, olive oil and eggs into a large mixing bowl and, using an electric hand-held mixer, whisk for a few minutes until you have a thick, golden cream that looks like pale, smooth custard.

7 Add the cocoa and coffee paste, keep whisking, then add the ground and chopped hazelnuts, chestnut flour and bicarbonate of soda and mix well.

8 Pour the batter into the lined cake tins. Bake for 40–50 minutes until just set on top and a skewer comes out fairly clean. Cool for a few minutes in the tins, then lift out and transfer to a wire rack to cool.

9 To assemble the cake, whip the cream with the vanilla. Place a wafer on the serving plate, spread on a little whipped cream and put a cake on top. Cover with more cream, the other cake and more cream. Top with the other wafer. Drizzle on a criss-cross of maple syrup to finish, if you like.

HOWARD'S TIP
Most supermarkets sell packets of roasted chopped hazelnuts, which are ideal for recipes like this.

LAPSANG MERINGUES

Makes 16–20 individual meringues (so 8–10 servings when sandwiched)

Tackling the egg / chicken puzzle of which came first, let's be honest – I came up with the name of this long before the recipe. It sounded good! Thankfully, it's not just a pretty name – as it turns out, adding tea to meringues actually works. Lapsang souchong provides a smoky setting for sharp lemon cream and the fragrant floral lychee. If this blend of tea just isn't your bag, try Earl Grey with fresh blackberries or perhaps rose pouchong with poached rhubarb. As you spoon the meringue mixture onto the baking sheet, try to keep them equal in size, but I don't worry too much about the shape. I reassure myself that it's in keeping to have a few trails that look like oriental calligraphy and the oddly shaped ones are just channelling their inner *netsuke*.

For the meringues	1½ tsp fine lapsang souchong tea	To serve
3 large egg whites (or equivalent pasteurised egg white)	(by coincidence, the contents of one tea bag!)	300ml double cream
75g icing sugar	1 tsp cream of tartar	finely grated zest of a large unwaxed lemon
75g soft brown sugar		10 fresh lychees (or a 425g tin of lychees in syrup, drained)

1 Preheat the oven to 120°C/100°C fan/gas ½ and line a baking sheet with baking parchment.

2 Whisk the egg whites in a large mixing bowl, using an electric hand-held mixer (or in the bowl of a stand mixer), until they form soft peaks.

3 In another bowl, sift the sugars with the tea, then add this a spoonful at a time to the egg whites, whisking on a medium speed until it's all incorporated.

4 Add the cream of tartar, then turn up the speed and whisk until the mixture is glossy and forms firm peaks.

5 Carefully spoon teaspoonfuls of the meringue onto the lined tray. Bake for 1 hour 40 minutes until cooked through and firm underneath. Leave on the baking parchment to cool.

6 When you're ready to serve, whisk the cream with the lemon zest until softly thick. Spoon on the flat side of a meringue, top with a slice or two of lychee and sandwich with another meringue.

HOWARD'S TIP

I find this recipe needs a teaspoon of cream of tartar to get the egg whites to thicken and peak. I don't know if it's the addition of tea or the use of pasteurised egg whites but it sometimes struggles to stiffen without.

HEDGEROW SUMMER PUDDING

Serves 6

'Hedgerow' for two reasons – firstly for its brambly mix of blackberries and rosehip (ignoring the less authentic strawberries and redcurrants), and secondly because this is perfect picnic fodder! Yes, after an overnight stint in the fridge, this pudding (still in its bowl, of course) is perfectly portable. I picture an entourage of EM Forster characters, venturing forth in crisp white linen to unmould the pudding in a summer meadow – the perfect (Howard's) end to a meal al fresco. In reality, the last time I did this was a drizzly Mother's Day at a soulless picnic park in Derbyshire.

The weighting process involved is not unlike pressing flowers. How lovely then to trap little fresh mint leaves against the side of the bowl. You could even use edible flower heads or petals, if so inclined. Frankly, it's a faff – gluten-free bread can be hard enough to handle without chasing errant foliage around a pudding basin. However, if you are of a mind to titivate for special occasions, it is a pretty touch. If your chosen bread is sturdy, you can dip it into the magenta juices before assembly – if fragile, best live with a gently dappled finish of pink and white and serve a jug of spare berry sauce on the side. Just when you thought this pudding couldn't be more summery, try stirring a little Sipsmith's Summer Cup into crème fraîche – the delicate blend of tea and cucumber is an idyllic August day on a dessertspoon.

225g blackberries

150g redcurrants, plus a sprig or two for decoration

300g strawberries, hulled and halved (or quartered, if very large)

2–3 tbsp rosehip syrup

a few small mint leaves or edible flower petals (optional)

about 400g white sliced gluten-free bread, crusts trimmed off

To serve

200ml crème fraîche

Sipsmith's Summer Cup, to taste

1 Put the fruit in a large saucepan with the rosehip syrup and heat gently until the berries soften and produce juice. Do not let it overcook and become too mushy. Take off the heat and leave to cool.

2 In a 1.2-litre (2-pint) pudding basin, press mint leaves or edible petals (if using) against the base and sides, then trap them by lining the basin with all but 2 slices of the bread, overlapping slightly so there are no gaps and leaving a little collar of bread at the top of the basin.

3 Fill the bread-lined basin with the fruit, saving the juices and any spare bits of fruit in a jug. Place the last couple of slices of bread on top of the fruit and carefully fold the collar of bread over, checking that there are no obvious gaps.

4 Place a small plate (or ideally the loose bottom from a 15cm (6in) cake tin) on top and then put a heavy weight on this (you can use a brick, cans of food or dumbbell weights from a long-forgotten fitness regime). Chill in the fridge, preferably overnight.

5 When ready to serve, mix the Sipsmith's with the crème fraîche. Remove the weights and plate and carefully slide a thin knife or palette knife around the edge of the pudding. Upturn onto a plate or cake stand and serve with the leftover juices and the crème fraîche.

HAZEL FLANN

Makes a 15cm (6in) flan

Yes I know you don't spell 'flan' like that but I created this dessert to mark my ~~Broadway~~, ~~London~~, Sheffield debut as the narrator of the forgotten musical, *Hazel Flagg*. It's a long story, but the lovely Dr Dominic McHugh was ~~foolish~~ kind enough to have faith in my 'interesting' voice. Anyway, this is a flan of the Spanish kind, similar to crème caramel. Usually the custardy crème has sugar added but since the hazelnut milk was already sweetened, I don't think it needs it. This has the added bonus of making the task of custard creation so much easier – no need to heat the milk, no fear of scrambling the eggs. I must admit that the science of this recipe baffles me – I'd originally hoped that the whole hazelnuts would stay welded to the caramel at the bottom of the tin so that it would turn out like a nutty upside-down cake. Instead, the hazelnuts part company from their amber adhesive and float to the top during baking. Equally bewildering, the caramel, that so resolutely sticks to the tin (and pan and spoon) when cold, does not firm up again after an overnight chill in the fridge but sweetly dissolves into a golden pond of sauce that releases the pudding from its tin with a satisfying plop, revealing a patently unblemished surface of shimmering gilded glossiness.

100g whole blanched hazelnuts	25g roasted chopped hazelnuts	1/2 tsp vanilla paste
100g caster sugar	3 large eggs	a small glass of hazelnut liqueur
a squeeze of lemon juice (about 1/2 tsp)	4 large egg yolks	(optional)
	600ml hazelnut milk	

1 Toast the whole hazelnuts for a minute or so in a hot pan (or in a baking tray in a hot oven) until lightly browned.

2 Preheat the oven to 140°C/120°C fan/gas 1.

3 Heat the sugar and lemon juice in a heavy-based saucepan over a low to medium heat until the sugar is dissolved. Watch it like a hawk. Resist the temptation to stir, though you can swirl the pan occasionally to encourage any dry patches of sugar to join the molten syrup. If sugar crystals appear on the sides of the pan (the lemon juice should help to prevent this), use a wet pastry brush to push these down.

4 When the syrup has turned a satisfying golden brown (it's personal taste how dark you go), you need to work swiftly, remembering that you are dealing with something that is as hot as hell.

5 Holding a 15cm (6in) cake tin (not loose-bottomed) with an oven glove, pour the caramel into the tin, then quickly tilt it so the base and lower sides are coated. Press the whole hazelnuts into the caramel and scatter the chopped nuts in between.

6 Whisk the eggs and egg yolks, then add the hazelnut milk and whisk this in along with the vanilla. Pour the mixture into the prepared tin.

7 Put a large roasting tin or deep baking tray into the oven and stand the filled cake tin in it. Pour hot water into the roasting tin to about 3cm (1¼in) deep so that it creates a bain-marie. Bake the pudding for about 2 hours until the surface is firm to touch but still wobbly like a jelly.

8 Leave to cool in the tin on a wire rack, then chill in the fridge overnight.

9 When you are ready to serve, take a thin sharp knife and carefully run it around the inner edge of the tin. Place a plate or cake stand on top, then upturn and wait for the sound of the suction release before lifting off the tin. Would it be gilding the lily to anoint with a little hazelnut liqueur? Well, in the spirit of *Hazel Flagg*, you only live once.

BACI DI UOMO

Makes about 50–60 biscuits, so 25–30 when sandwiched together

It's a fact of life that some people like a lady's kiss and some people like a gentleman's. (Worry not – this tale of cookie love gets no more explicit.) Taking the classic Italian *baci di dama* (lady's kisses), I butched them up a bit with a little espresso, a salted caramel filling and tiny dark chocolate moustaches. Cute as a button, these little creations are my way of ensuring there's equality and diversity in the biscuit tin.

For the biscuits
50g chopped almonds
50g roasted chopped hazelnuts
1/2 tsp instant espresso coffee
  powder
100g rice flour
75g caster sugar
75g unsalted butter, cut into small
  cubes

For the salted caramel
50g unsalted butter
120g caster sugar
50ml double cream
a generous pinch of sea salt
  (ideally *fleur de sel*) to taste

To decorate
25g dark chocolate

1 Begin by making the biscuits. Grind the almonds and hazelnuts in a nut grinder or food processor – you want them fairly finely ground but a few larger specks won't hurt.

2 Transfer the nuts to a large mixing bowl, along with the espresso powder, rice flour and sugar. Add the butter and rub this in as if making pastry. When the butter lumps have disappeared, start to bring the mix together, kneading forcefully until you have a cohesive ball of dough.

3 Be prepared for the next step to test your patience. Quarter the dough and carefully roll each piece into a smooth cylindrical sausage shape (noting that you want flat vertical ends, not tapering) about 2cm (³/₄in) in diameter. You may find that the dough sometimes crumbles and the cylinders refuse to stay smooth and intact, so it's a case of firmly coaxing … and sometimes re-rolling from scratch.

4 Place the rolls on a flat board lined with non-stick baking parchment (a small marble slab is perfect) and chill them in the fridge for at least 2 hours, or preferably overnight. (You may now feel ready for a lie down, a warm bath or a stiff drink – take it as your opportunity to chill too.)

5 Next, preheat the oven to 170°C/150°C fan/gas 3–4 and line two baking sheets with baking parchment.

6 With a sharp knife, cut the dough rolls into equal slices, about 1cm (¹/₂in) thick, and then gently roll each piece into a ball and place on the lined baking sheets.

7 Bake for 12–15 minutes until light golden brown. Leave the biscuits to cool completely, then store in an airtight tin until you're ready to fill them.

8 To make the salted caramel filling, put the butter and sugar in a small heavy-based pan over a medium heat and stir constantly with a wooden spoon until it becomes a smooth, dark caramel. It will go through several worrying stages, including sandy sludge and split sauce, but have patience and keep stirring. When the caramel is finally smooth and sufficiently dark for your taste, add the cream and stir like crazy. Take off the heat, stir in the salt and leave to cool.

9 Melt the chocolate in a heatproof bowl in the microwave (or in a bowl over a pan of simmering water), then spoon this into a disposable piping bag and snip the end so it has an opening of no more than 2mm ($^1\!/_{16}$in).

10 To assemble, sandwich the biscuits together with a little of the salted caramel, then pipe chocolate moustaches on their upper lips. Store in an airtight tin to keep them crisp. They'll soften over time but will last about 5 days – if there's no one in the house.

HEATON MESS

Makes at least 4 servings

I'm not sure if I was thinking here of the Heaton in Manchester or Yorkshire, but this is essentially a northern version of Eton mess, taking its flavour inspiration from the dark, sweet fruit of Chorley cakes and Eccles cakes. With the sweetness of both meringues and sauce, it really needs some tartness to balance it – try blackcurrants or slices of green apple. Lemon zest in the cream helps cut the sweetness, but you could also drop the cream in favour of a sharp grapefruit, lemon or yuzu sorbet.

For the meringues
3 large egg whites (or equivalent pasteurised egg white)
75g caster sugar
75g icing sugar

For the dark fruit sauce
75ml gluten-free beer (such as Green's Dark Ale)
25g dark soft brown sugar
50g currants
50g raisins
$1/2$ tsp mixed spice
1 tbsp date syrup

To serve
500ml double or whipping cream
grated zest of 1 lemon
about 170g blackcurrants or slices of apple

1 Preheat the oven to 120°C/100°C fan/gas $1/2$ and line a baking sheet with baking parchment.

2 To make the meringues, in a large mixing bowl, whisk the egg whites with an electric hand-held mixer until they form soft peaks. Add the caster sugar, a little at a time, whisking continuously, until the mixture is thick, glossy and stiff, then fold in the icing sugar with metal spoon.

3 Spoon teaspoons of the mixture onto the lined baking sheet and bake for 2 hours. Lift them off the baking parchment as soon as they are cool and store them in an airtight tin.

4 To make the sauce, heat the beer in a pan, add the brown sugar and let it dissolve. Add the currants, raisins and mixed spice and simmer for 5 minutes. Take off the heat, stir in the date syrup, then leave to cool.

5 To serve, whip the cream with the lemon zest until thick. Arrange the meringues, fruit and cream in little dishes and spoon over a little of the dark sauce.

HOWARD'S TIP
Date syrup is a natural sweetener, extracted (not surprisingly) from concentrated dates. Look out for jars or squeezy bottles of it in health food stores. You can make your own by cooking 10 dates in 250ml water until the water has reduced by half, then squeeze the dates through a sieve or conical strainer. Use it in place of honey or treacle for a little rich, dark fruitiness.

SATAY SUNDAES

Makes at least 4 servings

A deconstructed satay sauce in dessert form (where do I think these up from?), this includes coconut milk, chillies and lime, but I opted for cashews instead of the usual peanuts. Once made, the dairy-free ice cream can sit in the freezer and the cashew biscuits in a tin, ready for construction whenever you're ready, be that Satay night or Sundae morning.

For the chilli coconut ice cream
2 x 400ml cans of coconut milk
3 tbsp maple syrup
seeds from 3–4 cardamom pods
1/4 tsp fennel seeds
1/4 tsp dried chilli flakes

For the cashew chopsticks
1 large egg white (or equivalent pasteurised egg white)
50g icing sugar
grated zest of 1 lime
100g cashew nuts, roughly chopped

To serve
1 papaya
2 passion fruit
any other tropical fruit of your choice

1 Whisk together all the ice-cream ingredients, then pour the mixture into a shallow freezerproof dish or tub. Freeze for 45 minutes.

2 Take it out of the freezer and vigorously stir with a spatula or wooden spoon, bashing it about to break up any ice crystals. Pop it back in the freezer.

3 After 30 minutes, repeat the vigorous stirring and bashing, and do this every 30 minutes for the next 3 hours or so until you have achieved a good ice-cream consistency. You can now cover the ice cream and leave it in the freezer until you need it.

4 Preheat the oven to 160°C/140°C fan/gas 3 and line a baking sheet with baking parchment.

5 In a small mixing bowl, whisk the egg white with the icing sugar and lime zest just enough to break the egg white up a little. Add the chopped cashew nuts, and then spoon 8 trails of the mixture onto the lined baking sheet. You can tidy them up with wet fingers.

6 Bake for about 10–12 minutes until pale gold in colour. As soon as they come out of the oven, you can tidy up any rough edges with a sharp knife. Leave to cool and firm up on the baking parchment before you try to remove them. Store in an airtight tin until needed.

7 To assemble the sundaes, peel the papaya, remove its stone and use a melon baller to create little balls of fruit, (or you can just slice it) and place these in four sundae dishs. Add scoops of the coconut ice cream, passion fruit seeds and pulp, along with any other tropical fruit, and finish each with another scoop of ice cream. Top with two of the cashew chopsticks.

HOWARD'S TIP
Some people are sensitive to monodiglyceride so choose a coconut milk that doesn't have this as an emulsifier. Most coconut milks are just coconut and water but there are some brands that contain additives.

GOOSEBERRY BUSHES

Makes about 12 biscuit cups

The grown-up, dinner-party version of the *Ginger and honey coracles* (see page 90), these elegant biscuit cups contain a deliciously sharp gooseberry fool. The level of effort you put into making these tree-like is your call – I drew a leafy template and cut out the biscuits by hand, but stamp them out with a large pastry cutter if you have better things to do with your time. You can also literally raise them to another level by creating 'tree-trunks' of stacked mini biscuits, held together with melted dark chocolate. If the thought of such artistic endeavour sends you running for the woods, then feel free to trim your bush construction accordingly.

For the biscuits
230g rice flour, plus extra for dusting
120g potato flour
2 tsp matcha or sencha green tea powder (optional but it adds a little authentic colour and flavour)
1 tsp bicarbonate of soda
1 tsp xanthan gum

^{1}/2 tsp Chinese five-spice powder
110g unsalted butter
125g caster sugar
1 large egg
4 tbsp elderflower cordial

For the filling
20g butter

350g cooking gooseberries, washed and topped and tailed
2 tbsp elderflower cordial
200g crème fraîche

To decorate (optional)
25g dark chocolate
a few dessert gooseberries

1 To make the biscuits, sift the flours, green tea powder, bicarbonate of soda, xanthan gum and five-spice powder together, then rub in the butter until the mixture is like fine breadcrumbs. Stir in the caster sugar.

2 Beat the egg with the elderflower cordial and pour this in. Stir in the liquid with a knife, and then knead it by hand in the bowl until it comes together as a soft dough. Wrap the dough in cling film and chill for at least 30 minutes, or until needed.

3 Pre-heat the oven to 190°C/170°C fan/gas 5 and place 12 paper muffin cases on the underside of a muffin tin.

4 Dust the work surface with rice flour and roll out the dough to a thickness of 6mm (about ^{1}/4in). It's easiest to do this in two batches and a doddle if you have a rolling pin that can be set to roll a specific thickness.

5 Cut out leaf-edged circles (or stamp them out using a round cutter) about 10cm (4in) in diameter. Place these on the prepared tin.

6 Bake for about 15 minutes until just beginning to brown. Remember, all biscuits firm up a little more on cooling. Allow to cool on the tin a little, then carefully peel off the paper muffin cases as soon as you can and leave the biscuits to finish cooling on a wire rack.

7 If you are going to the trouble of creating 'tree trunks' for your bushes, re-roll any remaining dough and cut out small circles about 3cm (1^1/4in) in diameter. Bake on a baking sheet lined with baking parchment for about 5 minutes until just beginning to brown. Slide the parchment off the baking sheet and leave the biscuits to cool on a wire rack.

8 Break the chocolate into pieces and put in a microwave-proof bowl. Microwave in 30-second blasts, stirring until melted (or you can do this over a pan of simmering water). Sandwich three small biscuits together with the melted chocolate, then use another blob of melted chocolate to attach a biscuit cup on top. Leave to set.

9 To make the filling, melt the butter in a large pan on a low heat. Add the gooseberries, cover and leave to cook for 5 minutes.

10 When pale yellowy green, take off the heat, squash a little with a spoon to release the pulp from the fruit, transfer to a bowl, add the elderflower cordial and leave to cool. When cool, stir in the crème fraîche and chill until ready to serve.

11 Spoon the gooseberry fool into the biscuit cups. Serve with a few dessert gooseberries if you like.

HOWARD'S TIP
Powdered green tea adds a delicate but distinctive flavour and colour to biscuits and cakes. Matcha is the finest, brightest green tea and has a price tag to match, while sencha is its darker green, somewhat cheaper cousin. If you're out to impress, then it has to be matcha, but sencha is fine for a jaded budget.

CHEESY BISCUITS
LEMON AND POPPY SEED THINS

Makes about 16 thins

Lemons, poppy seeds, ground almonds ... fairly standard baking ingredients, but usually in a cake. This time, they're transformed into a savoury biscuit with a touch of the tagine.

100g ground almonds	30g poppy seeds	2 small preserved lemons, finely
30g pistachios, chopped	50g feta or other similar white	chopped and any pips removed
60g gram flour, plus extra for	cheese	1 large egg, beaten
rolling	1–2 tsp ras el hanout spice blend	

1 Preheat the oven to 200°C/180°C fan/gas 6 and line a baking sheet with baking parchment.

2 In a large bowl, mix together the ground almonds, chopped pistachios, gram flour and poppy seeds. Roughly grate or crumble the cheese and add this to the mix, along with the ras el hanout and the chopped preserved lemons.

3 Add the beaten egg and mix well, stirring with a knife at first, then use your hand to gather and clump the dough together until it forms a ball of soft dough.

4 On a floured surface, roll out the dough to a thickness of 4mm (about $^1/_6$in). Cut out 3x10cm ($1^1/_4$x4in) rectangles and carefully transfer them to the lined baking sheet.

5 Bake for about 15 minutes until golden, then slide the biscuits onto a wire rack to cool.

CHEESY BISCUITS
SEEDY CRACKERS

Makes 20–24 crackers

Another good biscuit for cheese or dips – sesame, hemp and poppy seeds are here for the crunch, and you can use spice seeds like cumin, fennel or black onion seeds to add to the flavour.

30g hemp seeds

30g sesame seeds

110g quinoa flour

50g ground almonds

1 tsp spice seeds (caraway, cumin or coriander – whatever you prefer)

a pinch of salt

1 tbsp extra virgin olive oil

2 large eggs, beaten

3 tsp poppy seeds

1 Toast the hemp seeds and sesame seeds in a hot pan for a few minutes. If the hemp seeds start to pop, trap them with the lid and take off the heat.

2 Preheat the oven to 200°C/180°C fan/gas 6.

3 In a large mixing bowl, mix together the quinoa flour, ground almonds, sesame seeds, hemp seeds, whatever spice seeds you are using, and a pinch of salt. Add the olive oil and beaten eggs and mix well.

4 Take two large sheets of baking parchment and lay one of the sheets on the work surface. Tip the mixture into the centre and place the other sheet on top.

5 Roll out the dough between the two sheets of parchment until it is at least 30cm (12in) square and level all over. You'll be able to tell when the dough is thin enough – stop when you feel the hemp seeds cracking under your rolling pin.

6 Cut the dough into about 20–24 squares or rectangles. You can trim the outer edges (if you're a fan of uniformity) or leave them ragged.

7 Brush a little water along alternate edges and sprinkle with poppy seeds. Give them a final roll with the rolling pin, just to press the poppy seeds into the surface.

8 Now carefully transfer each cracker onto a baking sheet lined with baking parchment (re-use the top sheet used for rolling) and bake for 12–15 minutes until golden brown. Slide the crackers onto a wire rack to cool.

CHEESY BISCUITS
MUSTARD CREAMS

Makes 15–20 sandwiched biscuits

A double take on the classic custard cream, these savoury biscuits are great for a party. It's fun to make them look as much like the original as you can – a rectangular biscuit cutter really helps – but be warned, these definitely aren't for dunking!

For the biscuits	a pinch of cayenne pepper	For the filling
200g rice flour, plus extra for rolling	20g fresh Parmesan cheese, grated	100g full-fat cream cheese
100g potato flour	2 tbsp smooth French mustard	^{1}/$_2$ tsp English mustard powder
50g millet flour	1 large egg, beaten	
^{1}/$_2$ tsp xanthan gum	1–2 tsp cold water (optional)	
110g cold unsalted butter, diced	yellow mustard seeds, to decorate	

1 In a large mixing bowl, mix together the flours and xanthan gum. Rub in the butter until there are no visible lumps. Stir in the cayenne pepper and grated Parmesan and then add the French mustard and egg. Mix well with your hand until the dough comes together. If it seems very dry, add a little cold water. Wrap in cling film and pop it in the fridge for 30 minutes.

2 Preheat the oven to 200°C/180°C fan/gas 6 and line a baking sheet with baking parchment.

3 On a floured surface, roll out the dough to 4mm (about ^{1}/4in) thick. Cut out rectangles about 4x7.5cm (1^1/2x3in) and place them on the lined baking sheet. (It's worth looking out for a biscuit cutter this size, especially one with rounded corners.) You should get 30–40 biscuits in total.

4 Imprint half the biscuits with a pattern, decorate with mustard seeds and leave the rest plain.

5 Bake for about 12 minutes until pale golden brown. The biscuits sometimes puff up unpredictably, which is annoying when you're seeking uniformity, but such is the price you pay for their flaky texture.

6 Slide the biscuits onto a wire rack to cool.

7 When the biscuits are cold, mix the cream cheese with the mustard powder. Spoon it into a disposable piping bag and cut the end to form a 4mm (about ^{1}/4in) opening. Pipe a border of filling on the back of the plain biscuits, then sandwich with the decorated tops.

CHOCOLATE BEAR BUNS

Makes 12 buns

A little bear hug at the end of a meal – flavour the buns with peppermint extract and you're in for a treat that's far more rewarding than the standard after-dinner mint. If minty-fresh bears are not your thing, try other flavours – perhaps a bear with a little coffee breath, or orange extract for a more fruity bear.

For the buns
50g unsalted butter
50g dark chocolate, chopped
150g rice flour
50g chestnut flour
$1/2$ tsp xanthan gum
1 tsp gluten-free baking powder
$1/4$ tsp bicarbonate of soda
20g organic cocoa powder

75g dark soft brown sugar
a pinch of salt
2 large eggs
2 tbsp yogurt
100ml warm water
1 tsp vanilla bean paste
a few drops of peppermint extract
   (or coffee or orange)

For the buttercream
100g unsalted butter, softened
160g icing sugar
40g organic cocoa powder

To decorate
chocolate sprinkles or organic
   cocoa powder
a little white icing (ready-to-roll
   fondant or sugar paste)
12 large fresh blueberries

1 Preheat the oven to 180°C/160°C fan/gas 4 and line a 12-hole muffin tin with paper cases.

2 Put the butter and chopped chocolate in a heatproof bowl and microwave for 30 seconds, stir, and then microwave for another 30 seconds. Stir again and the butter and chocolate should have melted together. If not, pop it back in the microwave for another quick blast.

3 In a large mixing bowl, put the flours, xanthan gum, baking powder, bicarbonate of soda, cocoa powder, brown sugar and a pinch of salt. Mix together to combine. Make a well in the centre of the dry ingredients and pour in the melted butter and chocolate.

4 Beat the eggs and add them into the mix, stirring well, followed by the yogurt, warm water, vanilla paste and peppermint extract (or other chosen flavouring). Mix thoroughly to make a smooth batter.

5 Spoon the batter into the muffin cases and bake for about 20 minutes until a cake tester comes out clean. Leave to cool in the tin for a few minutes, then transfer to a wire rack to cool fully.

6 To make the buttercream, in a large mixing bowl, preferably using an electric hand-held mixer, beat the butter until smooth and creamy. Sift the icing sugar with the cocoa powder and add this to the butter, a little at a time, whisking continuously, until you have a smooth, light buttercream.

7 Spoon half the buttercream into a piping bag fitted with a large, plain round nozzle. Spread the rest of the buttercream on the 12 buns, and then dip them into the chocolate sprinkles or cocoa powder.

8 Pipe a line of buttercream half way down the centre of each bun, to form the bridge of the bear's nose, then two blobs for the ears. If your buttercream is firm enough, you should be able to squeeze the ears with your finger and thumb to shape them.

9 Roll tiny balls of white icing to make the eyes and use a thin wooden skewer to make the pupils of the eyes and a hole for the mouth. Buff a blueberry with a piece of kitchen paper to give your bear a shiny nose.

HOLLYWOOD WEDDING CAKE

Contrary to what my so-called friends may say, this is not the cake for my fantasy marriage to a certain Mr H, but a tribute to the artistry of a golden era, when a little sequin and sparkle could put a smile on anyone's face. The secret here is that the glitter of the decorations masks any less-than-perfect efforts in the icing, so you don't have to be a great decorator. Rather than prescribing a specific recipe for your cakes (I used the *All-star fruit cake* (see page 186) and increased the quantities accordingly), I'm suggesting you choose any cake you fancy. You can even take the basic mixtures for the *Black Forest brownies* (see page 170) or *Snowball cocktail cakes* (see page 166) and double or triple them. And you don't have to have the same cake for all three tiers. Just remember that the fruit cake will keep much longer so it can be prepared further ahead, but any sponge cakes will need to be fresh. If you're using the fruit cake, it's usual to have a layer of marzipan too. The quantities of icing are generous, but it's best to work with too much rather than too little. I used white fondant icing on the top and bottom tiers, with lilac for the middle, but it's up to you – black and white would be very stylish too.

For the decorations
icing sugar, for rolling
about 150g sugar florist paste
white edible glitter
magenta edible glitter

For the bottom tier
1 x 25cm (10in) cake of your choice
apricot jam, to glaze the cake before icing
icing sugar, for rolling
about 1kg marzipan (if using)
1.5kg ready-to-roll white fondant icing

For the middle tier
1 x 18cm (7in) cake of your choice
apricot jam, as above
icing sugar for rolling
about 700g marzipan (if using)
1 kg ready-to-roll lilac fondant icing

For the top tier
1 x 13cm (5in) cake of choice
apricot jam, as above
icing sugar for rolling
about 350g marzipan (if using)
500g ready to roll white fondant icing

For the royal icing
1 large egg white (or equivalent pasteurised egg white)
225g icing sugar, sifted
1 tsp lemon juice

You will also need
1 x cake stand or thick round cake board, 30cm or larger
1 x 20cm (8in) thin cake board
1 x 15cm (6in) thin cake board
10 x cake dowels, 10cm (4in) or longer (or 5 x cake dowels, 20cm (8in) or longer)

1 Start by making the sequins. On a work surface dusted with icing sugar, roll out the sugar florist paste as thinly as possible (this paste will roll extremely thin), and stamp out 15mm (^{5}/8in) circles, then transfer them to a board or tray lined with baking parchment. If you don't have a cutter this size, use a small icing nozzle or bottle top. For cakes this size you'll need at least 180 sequins, so keep re-rolling and stamping out. Leave the little circles to dry out for at least 24 hours.

2 To make the two hearts for the top of the cake, roll out a thin strip of sugar florist paste about 1x10cm (^{1}/2x4in). Place the strip on its edge, roll the ends in, and then pinch midway to form a heart. Repeat with another strip. Leave the hearts to dry out for at least 24 hours.

3 To cover the cakes with marzipan, warm the apricot jam in a small pan. Strain the warm jam through a small sieve or tea strainer to take out any pieces of fruit.

4 Take the largest cake and place it on its board or cake stand. Brush it all over with the warm jam.

5 On a work surface dusted with icing sugar, roll out the marzipan to 5mm (^{1}/4in) thick. Keep checking that the marzipan isn't sticking by sliding a large palette knife underneath. Lift the marzipan by rolling it back over the rolling pin, and then roll it onto the cake. Smooth it by using the rolling pin on top and your hands (or an icing smoother) on the sides. Trim the marzipan with a sharp knife.

6 Place the medium cake on its thin board, brush with jam and cover with marzipan as above. Repeat with the small cake. Leave the cakes to dry out, overnight if possible.

7 To cover the cakes with fondant icing, take the largest cake and brush it with a little water.

8 On a work surface dusted with icing sugar, roll out the icing to about 5mm (^{1}/4in) thick. Again, keep checking that the icing isn't sticking by sliding a large palette knife underneath. Lift the sheet of icing by rolling it back over the rolling pin, and then roll it onto the cake. Smooth it by using the rolling pin on top and your hands (or an icing smoother) on the sides. Trim the icing with a sharp knife.

9 Repeat with the medium and small cakes. Leave the cakes to dry out, overnight if possible.

10 Take the large cake and lightly mark out a circle on top, slightly smaller than the medium-sized cake. Push a cake dowel into the centre, until it touches the board underneath, mark a line where the level of the cake top is on the side of the dowel, pull out the dowel, and cut it to the mark. Push the cut dowel back into the cake. Repeat with another four dowels equally placed within the marked circle.

11 Take the medium cake and lightly mark a circle on top, slightly smaller than the smallest cake. Repeat the dowelling with another five dowels.

12 To make the royal icing, in a large mixing bowl, whisk the egg white with an electric hand-held mixer for about 30 seconds to loosen it up. Add the icing sugar, a little at a time, whisking constantly. When you have added all the icing sugar, scrape down the sides of the bowl with a spatula, add the lemon juice and whisk on high speed for about 5 minutes until the icing is stiff and holds its shape.

13 Transfer the royal icing to a disposable piping bag and snip the end to make an opening about 3mm (^{1}/8in) wide.

14 Put the edible glitters on separate small plates. Dampen a sequin disc with water (using a brush or piece of kitchen paper) on one side, then dip it, wet-side down, into the glitter. Pipe a blob of royal icing on the side of the large cake and place the glittered disc against it. You want two rows of 18 sequins equally placed on the side of the cake and another 18 equally placed around the circumference on top.

15 Repeat with the medium cake and then with the small cake, but only decorate the sides of the small cake. On top of the small cake, pipe two blobs of icing and place the two hearts on top.

16 Assemble by carefully placing the medium cake on top of the large one, and the small cake on top.

CHAPTER 5
FREE AND FESTIVE

It probably won't surprise you to hear that the festive season is my favourite time of year. Fine food, friends, family and masses of fabulousness – what more could you ask for? The recipes here include classics with a twist and some quirkier contributions, but don't hamper their use to Yule. Follow in the footsteps of Auntie Mame and get your skates on anytime you need a little Christmas.

SPICED CRANBERRY STOLLEN

SNOWBALL COCKTAIL CAKES

KUMQUAT AND ALMOND GALETTE

BLACK FOREST BROWNIES

STICKY FIGGY PUDDINGS

STILTON AND WALNUT BISCUITS

DECEMBER DACQUOISE

FIG, APPLE AND WALNUT MINCEMEAT WITH CALVADOS

FRANGIPANE MINCE PIES

CHERRY BERRY MINCEMEAT

CHRISTMAS IN BAKEWELL

ALL-STAR FRUIT CAKE

BERGAMOT MARMALADE

GINGERBREAD THEATRE

SPICED CRANBERRY STOLLEN

Makes a 12x18cm (4$\frac{1}{2}$x7in) stollen

Teff flour adds a little substance to gluten-free bread, but this soft dough is still a little tricky to handle. Baking it in a long loaf tin gives it structure and has the added advantage of cunningly disguising it as a tea loaf, so you can happily serve it at any time of the year!

For the fruit
150g dried cranberries
4–5 tbsp calvados (or other fruity spirit)
grated zest and juice of 1 orange
2 pieces of preserved stem ginger in syrup, drained and roughly chopped (about 30g)

For the dough
400g gluten-free bread flour
50g teff flour
2 tsp quick yeast

10 cardamom pods (use fewer if you prefer a weaker cardamom flavour), husks removed and seeds crushed
$\frac{1}{2}$ tsp ground ginger
$\frac{1}{2}$ tsp mixed spice
2 tbsp soft brown sugar
325ml hemp milk (or other non-dairy milk)
3 egg whites (save the yolks for the frangipane)
grated zest of 1 lemon
1 tsp lemon juice
6 tbsp mild and light olive oil, plus extra for greasing

For the frangipane
3 egg yolks
90g caster sugar
4 tbsp mild and light olive oil
a few drops of almond extract
120g ground almonds

To finish
1 tbsp mild and light olive oil
about 25g flaked almonds or roasted chopped hazelnuts
a little icing sugar

1 You'll need a 900g (2lb) loaf tin and a shallow baking tin the same width as (or a tad wider than) the length of the loaf tin. Line them both with baking parchment and brush lightly with oil.

2 Soak the cranberries in the calvados, orange zest and juice for a few hours, or overnight. Add the chopped stem ginger.

3 To make the dough, mix the flours, yeast, spices and sugar in a large mixing bowl.

4 Warm the hemp milk in a small pan on the hob or in a heatproof jug in the microwave. Add the egg whites, lemon zest and lemon juice and whisk together. Pour into the dry ingredients and stir with a wooden spoon to combine.

5 Add the olive oil, stir well, then spoon the sloppy mix into the lined baking tin. Cover with a clean cloth or cling film and leave to rise at warm room temperature for about an hour.

6 Preheat the oven to 220°C/200°C fan/gas 7.

7 Spoon the fruit mixture over the dough and gently press it into the surface.

8 Make the frangipane by whisking the egg yolks in a bowl with the sugar, oil and almond extract. Add the ground almonds and beat well to combine. Spread the frangipane over the fruited dough as evenly as possible, but don't worry if it doesn't cover the whole surface.

9 Now for the tricky bit. Take hold of the paper under one of the shorter edges and begin to ease the dough over itself, as if making a Swiss roll. As the dough is fairly soft, it needs careful coaxing. Carry on until you have rolled up the dough fully and it is roughly the same size as the loaf tin.

10 Swiftly lift the rolled dough into the tin. Drizzle the oil over the top, scatter the flaked almonds or hazelnuts on top and bake for about 50 minutes until golden brown and firm.

11 Remove from the tin and cool on a wire rack, covered with a clean tea towel. When cool, dust with icing sugar. Allow the loaf to cool completely (for a few hours or overnight) before slicing.

SNOWBALL COCKTAIL CAKES

Makes 12 cakes

This is the cake homage to the Snowball cocktail (advocaat, lemonade and a maraschino cocktail cherry) as made by my late great aunt, Auntie Olive. It's a wonderfully retro and unashamedly kitsch little bun that takes its inspiration in equal measure from the déclassé contents of her drinks cabinet and the cream cakes of 1960s parties. The cocktail cherries you buy in jars nowadays are depressingly labelled 'maraschino flavour' and probably haven't smelled so much as a boozy breath of the original liqueur. To get the authentic cherrystone flavour you may need to order it online, as I did, or feel free to substitute another tipple, like kirsch, or dispense with it as you wish. After all, this is my personal nostalgia trip – nobody's twisting your arm to join me … though you're very welcome!

For the maraschino cherries	For the cakes	For the advocaat cream
12 dried sour cherries	3 unwaxed lemons (about 250–275g in total)	200ml double cream (or whipping cream, if you prefer)
a shot glass of maraschino liqueur	4 large eggs	4 tbsp advocaat (or to taste!)
	150g caster sugar	
	125g ground almonds	
	50g gluten-free ground rice	
	1 tsp gluten-free baking powder	

1 Put the dried cherries in the maraschino liqueur, cover the glass with cling film and leave the cherries to steep overnight.

2 To make the cakes, put the lemons in a pan of cold water, bring to the boil, cover and simmer gently for at least an hour until the skin is very soft. Remove from the pan and leave until cool enough to handle.

3 Preheat the oven to 190°C/170°C fan/gas 5 and line a 12-hole muffin tin with paper muffin cases.

4 Chop the skin of the lemons fairly finely (though a few chunks won't be a problem) and mash the flesh until you have a pulpy mush, removing and discarding any pips on the way.

5 Whisk the eggs in a large mixing bowl, and add the sugar, ground almonds, ground rice and baking powder. Stir in the lemon mush – skin and all. Spoon the mixture into the lined muffin tin.

6 Bake for 25 minutes until golden brown and springy to the touch. Remove from the tin and leave to cool on a wire rack.

7 When ready to serve, whisk the cream with the advocaat until just thick enough to pipe. Transfer the cream to an icing bag, pipe it onto the cakes and then top with a maraschino-soaked cherry.

KUMQUAT AND ALMOND GALETTE

Serves 6–8

Like a huge Danish pastry (or a sweet deep-pan pizza), this festive treat makes the most of seasonal kumquats – tangy, olive-sized oranges that bring marmalade bitterness to contrast with the sweet nuttiness of the almonds. If kumquats aren't in season, try stoned fresh cherries or drained bottled ones. I bake this in a 30cm (12in) springform cake tin, but you could also use a large rectangular tray like a Swiss roll tin. Perfect for sharing as a mid-morning snack, this galette also works as an indulgent Christmas breakfast! It's dairy free too, so almost everyone can have a slice.

For the dough base
450g gluten-free white bread flour blend
2 tsp quick yeast
2 tbsp caster sugar
a pinch of salt
300ml non-dairy milk (like hemp or almond)
1 tsp vanilla bean paste
3 large egg whites (save the yolks for the filling)
6 tbsp mild and light olive oil, plus a little extra for greasing

about 250g kumquat spread (such as St Dalfour's) or orange marmalade

For the almond filling
3 large egg yolks
1 large egg
4 tbsp mild and light olive oil
75g caster sugar
150g ground almonds
a few drops of almond extract

For the topping
50–75g fresh kumquats, washed and thinly sliced
a handful of flaked almonds
a little icing sugar

1 Line a 30cm (12in) springform cake tin with lightly oiled baking parchment.

2 In a large bowl, mix together the flour, yeast, sugar and salt.

3 Warm the non-dairy milk with the vanilla bean paste in a pan on the hob or in a heatproof jug in the microwave, then beat in the egg whites until blended.

4 Pour the liquid into the dry ingredients and mix well, then add 6 tablespoons of oil and stir this in. Don't overbeat – remember it's essentially a bread, not a batter, and it's fine to have a little residual halo of oil around the dough.

5 Spoon the dough into the lined baking tin and level it out. Press down on the dough, from the centre to the edges, until the dough starts to spread up the sides of the tin and curls over to form a shallow rim, looking like the edge of a stuffed crust pizza. Work methodically and carefully (you may need to oil your hands a little) until you have a shallow rim all the way round the edge, effectively creating a flan case.

6 Cover the dough base with a clean tea towel and leave it to rise in a fairly warm place for about 30 minutes.

7 Preheat the oven to 220°C/200°C fan/gas 7.

8 While the dough is rising, mix the almond filling. Whisk the egg yolks, egg, oil and sugar, then stir in the almonds and almond extract with a wooden spoon.

9 When the dough has risen, carefully cover the base with the kumquat spread, then spoon the almond paste into the case and level it out. Gently press the kumquat slices into the filling, then scatter the flaked almonds in the gaps.

10 Bake for about 30 minutes until the top is golden brown and the base sounds hollow when tapped.

11 Leave to cool in the tin slightly, and then transfer to a wire rack. Dust with icing sugar before serving.

BLACK FOREST BROWNIES

Makes 15 brownies

Opinion is divided about what makes the perfect brownie – some like a light, moist, melt-in-the-mouth morsel, whilst others claim that squelchy denseness lies at the heart of a true brownie. These favour the former – delectably moist fruits-of-the-forest that employ a little woodland of trees in the ingredients list.

For the brownies
390g jar of black cherries in kirsch (or 425g tin of black cherries in syrup)
125ml kirsch (or syrup) from the cherries above
50g organic cocoa powder, sifted
180g light soft brown sugar

100ml mild and light olive oil, plus extra for greasing
50ml walnut oil
3 large eggs
100g Brazil nuts, roasted (see page 66) and ground in a nut grinder or very finely chopped
50g chestnut flour
1/2 tsp bicarbonate of soda

For decoration
25g icing sugar
15 hazelnuts
50g dark chocolate
gold or dark green edible glitter (check that the brand you use is gluten free)

1 Drain the cherries, reserving the liquid.

2 Preheat the oven to 180°C/160°C fan/gas 4 and line a 20x30cm (8x12in) baking tray with lightly oiled baking parchment.

3 Heat the kirsch or cherry syrup in a small pan on the hob or in a heatproof jug in the microwave until steaming. Measure out 125ml of the warm liquid, pour it into a small bowl and whisk in the cocoa powder to make a smooth paste.

4 Put the sugar, olive oil, walnut oil and eggs into a large mixing bowl and, using an electric hand-held mixer, whisk for a few minutes until you have a thick, golden cream that looks like pale, smooth custard.

5 Add the cocoa paste, keep whisking to incorporate, and then add the roasted, ground (or finely chopped) Brazil nuts, chestnut flour and bicarbonate of soda and mix well.

6 Scatter the drained cherries in the lined baking tray, then pour the batter on top. Bake for 35–40 minutes until just set on top and a wooden skewer inserted in the centre comes out fairly clean. Leave to cool for a few minutes in the tin, then lift it out and transfer it to a wire rack to cool.

7 When cool, cut it into 15 squares. To decorate, you can either just dust with icing sugar and drizzle randomly with melted chocolate or you can do something a little more in keeping with the festive forest theme.

8 Cut an oak leaf shape out of thin card (small enough to fit on a brownie square). Place this template on a brownie, dust lightly with icing sugar and then deftly remove to reveal a brown leaf in the white snow. Repeat this on the other brownies. Melt the chocolate in the microwave (or in a heatproof bowl over a pan of simmering water). To create gilded 'acorns', dip a hazelnut into the chocolate (just enough to coat half the nut), then into a saucer of edible glitter. Place one 'acorn' on each brownie.

STICKY FIGGY PUDDINGS

Makes four 7.5cm (3in) individual puddings

If your list to Santa includes a nut-free, dairy-free pud that's lighter than the traditional offering and low in refined sugar, this could be a Christmas gift with your name on it. It's worth tracking down chestnut flour, for its flavour and obvious seasonal connotations.
By all means add a little cinnamon or orange zest if you fancy, but you will lose some of the subtle chestnut taste as a result.
The caramel sauce takes just a few minutes to make – granted there's not a lot, but you really only need a little, don't you? If you crave indulgence you could add a scoop of (dairy-free) ice cream; if you crave alcohol you could anoint the puds with Marsala or brandy before pouring on the sauce … or just have a tipple on the side.
The puddings dome dramatically when baked, so trim them level if the sight of a wobbly bottom smacks too much of impending New Year diets.

For the puddings
3 tbsp mild and light olive oil, plus extra for greasing
100g chestnut flour, plus extra for dusting
150ml boiling water
2 tsp instant espresso powder
100g soft dried figs, roughly chopped

2 large eggs
75g coconut sugar
30g gluten-free ground rice
$^1/_2$ tsp gluten-free baking powder
$^1/_2$ tsp bicarbonate of soda
$^1/_2$ tsp xanthan gum

For the sauce
35g coconut sugar
2 tbsp date syrup
1 tsp vanilla bean paste
3 tbsp non-dairy milk, such as hemp or coconut

1 Preheat the oven to 180°C/160°C fan/gas 4. Prepare the tins by wiping the insides with a lightly oiled piece of kitchen roll, then dust with a little chestnut flour and shake off the excess.

2 Make the coffee with the boiling water and instant espresso powder, and then pour this into a small bowl with the chopped figs.

3 In a large mixing bowl, whisk the eggs with the oil and coconut sugar for a few minutes until frothy.

4 Add the chestnut flour, ground rice, baking powder, bicarbonate of soda and xanthan gum, along with the figs and all their coffee marinade, and mix well with a wooden spoon.

5 Divide the mixture equally among the prepared tins and place them on a baking sheet. Bake for about 25 minutes until well risen and firm on top and a cake tester inserted in the centre comes out reasonably clean.

6 Leave them in their tins for 5 minutes, then slide a thin knife around the inner rim of the tins and upturn the puddings onto a plate. Trim the bottoms to level them, if you like.

7 To make the sauce, heat the coconut sugar, date syrup and vanilla in a small pan over a low-medium heat until the sugar has dissolved. Add the non-dairy milk, bring to the boil, and then simmer until it thickens a little. Pour the sauce over the puddings.

STILTON AND WALNUT BISCUITS

Makes about 16 biscuits

A lovely crunchy biscuit with a great texture – the addition of polenta adds an oaty quality, without having to track down gluten-free oatmeal. The Stilton bubbles away alarmingly when they bake, but don't worry – they turn out fine in the end.

100g ground walnuts (ground as fine as possible using a food processor or nut grinder)

30g walnuts, chopped

60g gram flour, plus extra for rolling

30g polenta

50g mature blue Stilton or other strong cheese, roughly grated

freshly ground black pepper

1 tsp dried thyme

1 large egg, beaten

1 In a large mixing bowl, mix together the ground and chopped walnuts, gram flour, polenta, grated cheese, pepper and dried thyme.

2 Add the egg and mix well, using your hand to gather the mixture together until it forms a ball of soft dough. Wrap in cling film and pop it in the fridge for 30 minutes.

3 Preheat the oven to 200°C/180°C fan/gas 6 and line a baking sheet with baking parchment.

4 On a floured surface, roll out the dough to a thickness of 4mm (about $^{1}/_{4}$in). Cut out 6cm ($2^{1}/_{2}$in) circles and carefully transfer them to the baking sheet. By re-rolling you should get about 16 biscuits in total.

5 Bake for about 15 minutes, ignoring the little pools of oil (from the cheese and nuts) that escape from them.

6 Slide the biscuits onto a wire rack to cool.

DECEMBER DACQUOISE

Makes a 15cm (6in) cake

A dacquoise is traditionally made with almonds and hazelnuts, but this nut-free dessert uses coconut in the meringue discs. A tinge of rosewater in the brittle icicles hints at the temptation of Turkish Delight – a nod to a Narnian winter. Stacked with whipped cream and fresh berries, and topped with a fragile icicle forest, this is both magical and manageable. Store the meringues in airtight tins and they'll keep fresh and crisp for days – let them get a whiff of moisture and they'll soften in seconds. Keep the construction until the last minute to avoid a flaccid finish. Choose a fresh red fruit with a little sharpness – redcurrants, pomegranate seeds or baked rhubarb – or go for a snow-covered Black Forest with preserved cherries. Though this makes a stunning Christmas centrepiece, it could easily be adapted for a winter wedding cake, though you may decide to replace the icicles with stiff shards of white chocolate if the only droop you want to see is the drupe of the coconut.

For the icicles
2 large egg whites (or equivalent pasteurised egg white)
^{1}/2 tsp cream of tartar
50g caster sugar
a few drops of rosewater
50g icing sugar, sifted

For the dacquoise discs
5 large egg whites (or equivalent pasteurised egg white)
225g caster sugar
2 tsp cornflour
2 tsp lemon juice
75g icing sugar, sifted
75g desiccated coconut

For the filling
600ml double cream or whipping cream
about 300g fresh berries, baked rhubarb or pomegranate seeds (or a mix)

1 First make the meringue icicles. Preheat the oven to 120°C/100°C fan/gas ½ and line a baking sheet with baking parchment.

2 Using an electric hand-held mixer, whisk the egg whites with the cream of tartar in a large mixing bowl until it forms soft peaks.

3 Add the caster sugar a little at a time, whisking continuously, until the egg whites are thick, glossy and stiff. Add the rosewater, and then fold in the sifted icing sugar with a metal spoon.

4 Transfer the mix to a piping bag fitted with a closed star nozzle. Pipe the icicles onto the lined baking sheet – start at the back, squeezing the bag firmly, then release the pressure as you bring the bag towards you, so each icicle starts thick and trails off.

5 Bake for 2 hours, then turn off the heat and leave them in the oven as it cools for a further 1 hour. Bring them out to cool at room temperature, but as soon as they are fully cooled, carefully remove them from the baking parchment and get them into an airtight tin.

6 Now make the dacquoise discs. Preheat the oven to 140°C/120°C fan/gas 1. Cut five 15cm (6in) circles of baking parchment (or you can used pre-cut parchment circles for lining cake tins) and place them on two baking sheets.

7 In a large mixing bowl, whisk the egg whites until they form stiff peaks, then add the caster sugar a little at a time, whisking continuously until the egg whites are glossy, thick and stiff. Whisk in the cornflour and lemon juice, then fold in the sifted icing sugar and coconut with a metal spoon.

8 Divide the mixture equally among the circles of baking parchment, coaxing it to the edges and levelling it off with the back of your spoon or a spatula.

9 Bake for 1 hour, then turn off the heat and leave them in the oven as it cools for a further 1 hour. Bring them out to cool at room temperature – get them into an airtight tin as soon as you can.

10 To assemble, whip the cream until it holds its shape. Carefully peel the parchment circles from the back of the dacquoise discs. Place one of the discs on a cake board or platter, spread whipped cream on top, scatter with fruit, place another disc on top and repeat. Finish with a layer of cream and berries, then push the icicles upright into this to form a forest.

FIG, APPLE AND WALNUT MINCEMEAT WITH CALVADOS

Makes enough for at least 24 mince pies

This suet-free mincemeat is a great way of trying out unusual liqueurs ... or using up the leftovers. Here I cooked the fruit in elderberry port, then added Calvados (apple brandy) at the end, but anything similar will do the job.

A word about mixed spice – supermarket fare usually consists of some combination of cinnamon, coriander, ginger and cloves, but venture further afield and you'll find star anise, cardamom and many more. Try independent shops or use a spice grinder and create your own blend.

75ml elderberry port	75g dried figs, chopped	30g walnuts, roughly chopped or
75g dark soft brown sugar	75g raisins	broken
1 medium-sized Bramley apple,	30g currants	2 tbsp date syrup
peeled, cored and grated	2 tsp mixed spice	about 75ml Calvados

1 Heat the port in a large pan, add the sugar and let it dissolve.

2 Add the grated apple, figs, raisins, currants and mixed spice. Simmer vigorously for about 15 minutes until the apple begins to soften and most of the liquid is absorbed.

3 Stir in the walnuts and date syrup, then take off the heat and add most of the Calvados.

4 Spoon into a sterilised jar, let it cool a little, and add a final glug of Calvados before putting the lid on.

> **HOWARD'S TIP**
> To sterilise glass jars, wash them in hot soapy water, rinse with hot water, dry with a clean tea towel, then pop them in a medium oven (about 180°C) for 5–10 minutes. If you are using jars with metal lids, sterilise them by boiling in a pan of water. If you use jars with rubber seals (like Le Parfait or Kilner jars), clean the seals in boiling water too. Before using, always check that there are no cracks or chips in your jars.

FRANGIPANE MINCE PIES

Makes 10–12 large pies using a muffin tin – more if you use a shallow tart tin.

This is very soft dough to handle, so keep it cool and use plenty of rice flour on the work surface and rolling pin. For a citrusy Christmassy decoration, I use slices of preserved kumquat from a local Chinese supermarket – if they're in season, you could use halved fresh kumquats or miniature clementines, or finish with strands of fresh orange zest.

For the pastry
150g rice flour, plus extra for rolling
50g quinoa flour
50g ground almonds
50g icing sugar
a pinch of salt
1/4 tsp gluten-free baking powder
125g cold unsalted butter, diced
1 tsp grated lemon zest
1 large egg
1 large egg white (save the yolk for the frangipane)

For the filling
1 large egg
1 large egg yolk
90g caster sugar
4 tbsp mild and light olive oil
120g ground almonds
1/2 tsp of almond extract
12 tsp mincemeat (about 200g)

To decorate
slices of preserved kumquats

1 To make the pastry, put the flours in a large mixing bowl and add the ground almonds, icing sugar, salt and baking powder. Rub the butter into the dry ingredients until there are no visible lumps, then stir in the lemon zest.

2 Beat the egg with the egg white and add this to the mix. Stir this in with a knife to begin with, and then gather the dough together using your hand. Wrap the dough in cling film and chill it in the fridge for about 30 minutes.

3 On a well-floured surface, roll out the chilled dough to about 5mm (1/4in) thick (it's easiest to do this by rolling half the dough, then repeating with the other half). Stamp out 10 to 12 circles using a 10cm (4in) round cutter and carefully line the muffin tin.

4 Chill for another few minutes (in the fridge or freezer) while you mix the frangipane. Preheat the oven to 210°C/190°C fan/gas 6–7.

5 Make the frangipane by beating the egg with the caster sugar and oil. Add the ground almonds and almond extract and mix well with a wooden spoon.

6 Put a spoonful of mincemeat in each pastry shell, and then top with frangipane and finally a slice of preserved kumquat. Bake for 15–20 minutes until the pastry is cooked and the frangipane is golden brown. Leave to cool a little before removing from the tins to finish cooling on a wire rack.

CHERRY BERRY MINCEMEAT

Makes enough for at least 24 mince pies

A different take on mincemeat that's more like a sharp, indulgent cherry jam. Traditional vine fruits make way for both glacé and sour cherries, with fresh cranberries providing pectin.

75ml sherry

75g light brown muscovado sugar

300g cranberries

150g glacé cherries, halved

75g dried sour cherries

30g dried blueberries

1 tsp star anise powder

2 pieces of preserved stem ginger in syrup, drained and chopped (about 30g)

2 tbsp syrup from the jar of stem ginger

about 75ml kirsch, maraschino liqueur or cherry brandy

1 Heat the sherry in a large pan, add the sugar and let it dissolve.

2 Add the cranberries, glacé cherries, sour cherries, blueberries and star anise powder. Simmer for about 10 minutes until the cranberries begin to pop and most of the liquid is absorbed.

3 Take off the heat, stir in the chopped stem ginger and its syrup and add most of the kirsch (or other cherry-based alcohol of choice).

4 Spoon into a sterilised jar and add a final glug of kirsch before sealing the lid.

CHRISTMAS IN BAKEWELL

Makes 12 tarts

I'm likely to distress the good people of Bakewell by coming up with this recipe. They're very proud and particular about their famous product – theirs is a pudding not a tart, whereas this one is definitely more of the tarty variety.

You can bake this as 12 mince pies in a muffin tin but it also works as a tray bake or as one large tart (follow the instructions for the *Seville orange tart* (see page 134) and increase the baking time accordingly). If you want to adapt this for a spring or summer in Bakewell, replace the mincemeat with fresh cherries or raspberries and a squirt of rosehip syrup.

For the pastry

150g rice flour, plus extra for rolling

50g millet flour

50g coconut flour

50g icing sugar

a pinch of salt

$^1/_4$ tsp gluten-free baking powder

$^1/_4$ tsp guar gum

125g cold unsalted butter, diced (or dairy-free spread)

1 tsp grated lemon zest

1 large egg

1 large egg white (save the yolk for the topping)

For the topping

125g unsalted butter, softened (or dairy-free spread)

125g caster sugar

125g rice flour

$^1/_2$ tsp gluten-free baking powder

$^1/_2$ tsp xanthan gum

2 large eggs

1 large egg yolk

30g gluten-free ground rice (optional)

1 tsp vanilla extract (or vanilla bean paste)

For the filling

12 tsp Cherry berry mincemeat (about 200g)

a little Demerara sugar to finish (optional)

1 To make the pastry, put the flours in a large mixing bowl and add the icing sugar, salt, baking powder and guar gum. Rub the butter into the dry ingredients until there are no visible lumps, then stir in the lemon zest.

2 Beat the egg with the egg white and add this to the mix. Stir it in with a knife to begin with, and then gather the dough together using your hand. Wrap the dough in cling film and chill it in the fridge for about 30 minutes.

3 On a well-floured surface, roll out the chilled dough to about 5mm ($^1/_4$in) thick (it's easiest to do this by rolling half the dough, then repeating with the other half). Stamp out 10 to 12 circles using a 10cm (4in) round cutter and carefully line the muffin tin.

4 Chill for another few minutes (in the fridge or freezer) while you mix the topping. Preheat the oven to 210°C/190°C fan/gas 6–7.

5 In a large mixing bowl, cream the butter with the caster sugar.

6 In a separate bowl, sift the rice flour with the baking powder and xanthan gum.

7 Beat the eggs and egg yolk and add this, a little at a time, alternating with the flour. Stir in the ground rice, then add the rest of the flour and the vanilla and mix well.

8 Put a spoonful of the mincemeat in each pastry case, spoon the cake mix equally on top, then sprinkle with Demerara sugar.

9 Bake for 15–20 minutes until the pastry is cooked and the sponge is golden. Leave to cool a little before removing from the tins to finish cooling on a wire rack.

ALL-STAR FRUIT CAKE

Makes a 20cm (8in cake)

This classic fruit cake is not just for Christmas – it will see you through all sorts of family celebrations, from weddings to birthdays. Keep to the same ratio of ingredients and just double (or triple) the ingredients if you want to bake a bigger cake or more than one. Of course, you don't need the excuse of a celebration – it's a keeper, so it can last for weeks of teatime treats.
I like chunky slivers of mixed peel, rather than the finely chopped stuff in tubs – it's worth tracking down whole pieces of candied peel. Feel free to use any marmalade but my home-made bergamot marmalade (see page 188) is a nice addition.
To create the star pattern on top of the cake, use extra glacé cherries and stem ginger pieces with whatever nuts you fancy.

350g sultanas

100g raisins

50g currants

50g glacé cherries

3 pieces of preserved stem ginger in syrup, drained and sliced (about 50g)

50g candied peel, cut into thick slivers

100ml brandy or Marsala wine, plus extra for feeding (see note for alcohol-free version)

125g unsalted butter (or dairy-free spread), plus extra for greasing

110g dark soft brown sugar

grated zest of 1 lemon

grated zest of 1 clementine

130g rice flour

70g potato flour

2 tsp mixed spice

1 tsp gluten-free baking powder

1 tsp xanthan gum

3 large eggs

60g ground almonds

2 tbsp marmalade

1 Put the sultanas, raisins, currants, glacé cherries and peel in a large mixing bowl and pour over the brandy. Stir, cover and leave overnight, or until you're ready to mix the cake.

2 Preheat the oven to 160°C/140°C fan/gas 3. Lightly grease a 20cm (8in) springform cake tin and line it with a double layer of baking parchment, coming up about 10cm (4in) above the rim of the tin.

3 In a large mixing bowl, cream the butter and sugar until light and fluffy, then beat in the lemon and clementine zests.

4 In a separate bowl, sift together the flours, mixed spice, baking powder and xanthan gum. Add the eggs, one at a time, alternating with the flour, and mixing well after each addition. Add any remaining flour and the ground almonds and mix well.

5 Stir in the dried fruit and its soaking liquid, along with the marmalade, and mix until everything is incorporated.

6 Bake for about 1½–2 hours until a skewer inserted in the middle comes out clean.

7 Immediately pour over a good glug of brandy and cover with foil to trap the steam. Leave the cake to cool in the tin. When cold, wrap in foil and store in an airtight tin. You can 'feed' it with another glug of brandy occasionally if you're keeping the cake for a special occasion.

8 Brush the surface with melted apricot jam or stem ginger syrup before decorating.

HOWARD'S TIPS

For an alcohol-free version, soak the dried fruit in something festive like cranberry juice or orange juice, and instead of feeding it with more booze, use the syrup from the jar of stem ginger.

For a nut-free version, replace the ground almonds with desiccated coconut or ground rice and don't use any nuts if you decorate the top.

BERGAMOT MARMALADE

Makes enough for a 500ml jar

Bergamots are only around for a few months, so make the most of them while you can. I've recently discovered somewhere that sells culinary grade bergamot oil, so at least I can get my fix when they're no longer in season.

3 bergamots (about 400g)

juice of a lemon

500g preserving sugar

1 Wrap each bergamot in a little piece of muslin (or a clean hankie) and tie with string. This will help to stop the precious bergamot juices and flesh from escaping into the water when it is cooked.

2 Put the wrapped bergamots in a large pan and fill with enough water so they float. Bring to the boil and simmer for about $1^{1}/_{2}$–2 hours. You can unwrap one and have a look after an hour to see if the skin is soft enough. Try to leave them cooking for as long as possible, but not to the point of disintegration.

3 When cooked, unwrap the bergamots, chop the skin into thin slivers and put this and the flesh into a pan. Keep an eye out for any pips and pick them out.

4 Add the lemon juice and sugar and cook gently to dissolve the sugar, then turn up the heat and let it boil for about 10 minutes until you reach setting point. (Test a blob of the marmalade on a cold plate and it is ready when it wrinkles when pressed.)

5 Spoon into a sterilised jar, let it cool, and then seal the lid.

GINGERBREAD THEATRE

Makes a 22x9cm (8^1/$_2$x3^1/$_2$in) theatre

Simpler to make than most gingerbread houses and just that bit more ... theatrical. It's actually easier than it looks – apart from the proscenium swags, most of the biscuits are square or rectangular, and it's your call how much detail goes on the stage – keep it sparse and Pinteresque or go all out and indulge your latent Ziegfeld.
I like the simple contrast of pure white on ginger biscuit, but you could colour the icing if you prefer and add sweets and edible glitter – just make sure you check that all decorations are gluten free.

For the biscuits
460g rice flour, plus extra for rolling
240g potato flour
2 tsp bicarbonate of soda
2 tsp xanthan gum
4 tsp ground ginger

220g cold unsalted butter, cut into small cubes (or use dairy-free sunflower spread)
340g dark soft brown sugar
2 large eggs
4 tbsp date syrup
4 tbsp syrup from a jar of stem ginger

For the royal icing
1 large egg white
225g icing sugar
^{1}/$_2$ tsp lemon juice

1 Using squared paper, cut out the following templates:
Large square 19x19cm (7^1/$_2$in)
Medium rectangle 4.5x16cm (1^3/$_4$x6^1/$_4$in)
Thin rectangle 3x19cm (1^1/$_8$x7^1/$_2$in)
Fancy proscenium 22cm (8^3/$_4$in) wide and about 9cm (3^1/$_2$in) at its tallest point. You can draw swags and tails at the bottom and a pediment at the top – make it as simple or as fancy as you like.

2 To make the gingerbread, sift the flours into a large mixing bowl and add the bicarbonate of soda, xanthan gum and ground ginger. Rub in the butter (or sunflower spread) until the mixture is like fine breadcrumbs, and then stir in the brown sugar.

3 Beat the eggs with the date syrup and ginger syrup, and then pour this into the dry ingredients. Stir in the liquid with a knife, and then knead it by hand until the mixture comes together as a soft dough. Wrap the dough in cling film and chill for at least 30 minutes, or until needed.

4 Preheat the oven to 190°C/170°C fan/gas 5 and line two baking sheets with baking parchment.

5 Dust the work surface with rice flour and roll out the dough to 6mm (about ^{1}/$_4$in) thick. It's easiest to do this in four batches and it's a doddle if you have a rolling pin that can be set to roll to a specific thickness.

6 Cut out 2 large squares. Leave one of the squares plain. If you're planning to have working footlights in your theatre, stamp out three small circles using a 15–20mm (^{1}/$_2$–^{3}/$_4$in) cutter near the edge of one side of the other square. Transfer them to a lined baking sheet and bake for about 15–18 minutes. As soon as the biscuits come out of the oven, trim them with a sharp knife while they are still warm, using the 19cm (7^1/$_2$in) square template again. Slide them onto a wire rack to cool and firm up.

7 Cut out 4 medium rectangles. Transfer them to a lined baking sheet and bake for about 12–15 minutes. There is no need to trim these fully, but you will find it easier to construct the theatre if you trim one of the short edges on each biscuit while they are still warm. Slide them onto a wire rack to cool and firm up.

8 Cut out 4 thin rectangles. Transfer them to a lined baking sheet and bake for about 12–15 minutes. Trim them with a sharp knife while still warm, then cool on a wire rack.

9 Cut out 1 fancy proscenium. You can cut decorative openings in this using little cutters – I used a star and a heart. Transfer it to a lined baking sheet and bake for about 15–18 minutes. Don't trim back the edges but you may want to re-use the little cutters while it is still warm, to sharpen up the decorative openings.

10 You can put whatever decorative scenery and characters you want on the stage. I made simple triangular tree shapes and a slightly rough-looking fairy godmother. You can also stamp out 3 stars to mask the footlights. Bake for about 12–15 minutes depending on size.

11 When the biscuits are cool, store them in airtight tins until you're ready to construct the theatre.

12 To make the royal icing, put the egg whites in a large mixing bowl and whisk with an electric hand-held mixer for about 30 seconds until loosened up. Gradually add the icing sugar, a little at a time, whisking continuously. Add the lemon juice, and then scrape down the sides of the bowl with a flexible spatula.

13 Keep whisking for about 5 minutes until the icing is stiff and holds its shape. You can use this immediately or keep it in an airtight tub in the fridge until needed.

14 To construct your theatre, take a large cake board, bigger than 23cm (9in) square. I used a round board 35cm (14in) in diameter. Put the large square template in the centre of the board and draw around it with a pencil.

15 Put a couple of spoonfuls of the royal icing in a piping bag – don't overfill it, as it's best to top up as needed. I use a disposable bag and snip the end so it has an opening of no bigger than 2mm.

16 Take 2 of the medium rectangles and pipe vertical lines on them – these are the side curtains. Decorate the fancy proscenium. Place it on top of the curtains, with a generous blob of icing under each end. Leave this to set completely.

17 Take the plain large square and decorate to make the backdrop. I just piped lots of dots to give a snowy sky effect.

18 Now take 3 of the thin rectangular biscuits. Put them upright on their long edges on the cake board, so they border three sides of the square you've drawn. These will form the support for the stage. You may need to trim the short edges a little so they fit in the square. Place the square stage biscuit on top, just to check it fits.

19 Pipe a generous amount of icing on the back of the rear biscuit. Press the backdrop against it, so it stands upright. Put a jar or mug behind it to hold it in place while the icing sets. Take the two remaining medium rectangles and fix them with icing on the sides of the stage, at the front.

20 When you are confident that these have set (use jars or mugs again to hold them until they do), pipe icing down the front edges and press the proscenium and curtains against them. Hold this in place with mugs and pipe more icing down the seams to seal any gaps and make absolutely sure everything will hold in place.

21 Using a sharp serrated knife, trim the last thin rectangle so it bridges the gap at the front of the stage.

22 Decorate the 3 stars, pipe a blob of icing on the backs and stick them on this biscuit.

23 Decorate the scenery and characters and stick them on them on the stage. Finally, remove all the jars and mugs you've had holding things in place.

24 You can light up the front of the stage with three battery tea lights. Slip them under the front of the stage (lift the stage up if necessary) and mask the footlights with the 3-star biscuit.

ACKNOWLEDGEMENTS

Thank you to everyone who shares my love of food … and makes me laugh. To fabulous foodie friends – Stella Morgan, Jo Peck, Phil Reid, Gavan Knox and Michelle Houston. To my fellow members of the bakers' dozen – Ali, Beca, Christine, Deborah, Frances, Glenn, Kimberley, Lucy, Mark, Rob, Ruby, and Toby. Thanks to Heather and Jack at HHB, Nikki, Giles and Clive at Little, Brown, Julie and Chris at Hartingtons and to Tallulah for being so enthusiastic about the idea that my first TV bake should be gluten-free. A big thank you to Wendy Hobson for being such a wonderfully helpful and constructive editor. Thank you to supportive work colleagues – Sarah, Teresa, Kay, Chris, Simon and Anne. Huge thanks to Darren Williams for his invaluable hospitality in selflessly providing a London base when I needed it, and for his priceless friendship. Thank you to my wonderful, inspirational family – my Mum and Dad, who've happily tested more bakes than anyone should have to do, to the brilliant Butterfields – Debbie, Rob, Coral, Lola and Violet – and to my beloved Peter, who has shown more patience than I thought humanly possible. I promise things will get back to normal … sometime very soon.

INDEX